S0-ABR-814

06/24
STRAND PRICE
$ 5.00

This Book Is for You If ...

This book is for people who have encountered despair, who have felt lost and alone in a broken world of chaos and darkness. This book is for you if:

- You are suffering from an illness or injury that has left you shattered, aware of your vulnerability;
- You have been wounded by betrayal in love, profession, or family that has made life seem uncertain and unsafe;
- A loved one is struggling with despair and you wish to offer a compassionate presence;
- You care for those who are in pain, as a member of the clergy, a medical professional, or a devoted friend, and the burdens appear at times to be overwhelming;
- A recent trauma has turned the world into a place of sorrow or you have lived for some time with the sense that the world is not quite right;
- You have lost a loved one to death, whether by illness, accident, or suicide, and you are struggling with anger, guilt, and fear;
- You yearn to make suffering meaningful and are willing to process the loss to live with humility and gratitude ...

Healing from Despair: Choosing Wholeness in a Broken World is written with the hope that you will come to see yourself as a blessing to others in a world that is at once broken and good. Although grounded in Jewish life and learning, it is a description of the human condition and is meant to give comfort and insight to people of all faiths.

Praise for *Healing from Despair: Choosing Wholeness in a Broken World*

"Rabbi Elie Kaplan Spitz's warm and sensitive meditations on hope and despair, joy and melancholy, faith and loss of faith will certainly appeal to religious students and secular readers alike."

—**Elie Wiesel**

"A moving and very personal exploration of the dark side of life. For those in trouble, Rabbi Spitz walks before us with a lamp of learning, illuminating a compassionate path."

—**Rabbi David Wolpe**, rabbi of Sinai Temple in Los Angeles, California; co-author of *Making Loss Matter: Creating Meaning in Difficult Times*

"A work of deep strength, comfort, and hope. Rabbi Elie Spitz teaches us that we are far more resilient than we even imagined. He gently raises us out of despair, reminding us that we are never alone in our suffering. Stories of uplift heal our souls, and practical tools renew our faith in ourselves, in our loved ones and in our God. Rabbi Spitz offers us a path to *tikkun* (repair). May his words lead us to the repair we seek."

—**Rabbi Naomi Levy**, author of *To Begin Again* and *Talking to God*

"A gift for individuals struggling to move onward and upward from the depths of despair. Readers will discover hope, solace, and practical advice on how to transcend their darkest moments. A soulful roadmap for those yearning for the wisdom and empathy of others who have 'been there' in repairing the world."

—**Jerry White**, co-founder of Survivor Corps; author of *I Will Not Be Broken: Five Steps to Overcoming a Life Crisis*

"More than a roadmap for life renewed, it is a compass pointing us back toward love, joy, and meaning. Rabbi Spitz speaks with the wise voice of a sage who has enhanced his harrowing experience with the riches of an ancient and sacred tradition. We walk with him into paths of deepest despair and poignant loneliness, and then, inspired by his caring courage, he walks us back into the light, back on to the path. We emerge strongest where once we were broken. This in no mere book—it is a lifeline."

—**Rabbi Bradley Shavit Artson**, dean of the Ziegler School of Rabbinic Studies and vice president, American Jewish University; author of *Gift of Soul, Gift of Wisdom: A Spiritual Resource for Mentoring and Leadership*

"Elie Spitz's inspired healing from deep suffering engenders in us hope and power to learn from him. He is sublime, earthy and pitilessly honest. Significantly, the universal and the Jewish are one."

—**Jacob Milgrom**, Professor Emeritus of Biblical Studies, University of California at Berkeley and **Dr. Jo Milgrom**, Schechter Institute of Jewish Studies, Jerusalem; author, *Handmade Midrash*

"This is a hard book—and that is what draws the reader into it. No quick fixes. No easy answers. Only straight wisdom that comes from the deepest recesses of the soul. This is also a deeply moving and profound book, filled with individual *kavannot* (sacred mantras) that cause the reader to pause and reflect. And this is a book of courage, for it is essentially the tale of a spiritual leader who got lost in the narrow places of Egypt and found his way to the Land of Promise."

—**Dr. Kerry M. Olitzky**, executive director of the Jewish Outreach Institute; author of *Grief in Our Seasons: A Mourner's Kaddish Companion*

"If all Rabbi Elie Spitz had done with the book *Healing from Despair* is to provide a vivid description of despair, based on his personal travail, it would have been a major contribution. But Rabbi Spitz goes further and, drawing on his own experience, shows that the awesome sense of despair and feeling utterly useless can be actually be the seed from which a sense of purpose and meaning, indeed a sense of mission, can sprout."

—**Rabbi Abraham J. Twerski, MD**, psychiatrist; author of *Happiness and the Human Spirit: The Spirituality of Becoming the Best You Can Be* and *Waking Up Just in Time*

"'You turned my depression to happiness; you took off my rags and wrapped me in joy' (Psalm 30). Rabbi Elie Spitz in sharing his own journey and in the way he offers effective counsel can make this quote from Psalm 30 become your truth."

—**Rabbi Zalman Schachter-Shalomi**, author of *First Steps to a New Jewish Spirit: Reb Zalman's Guide to Recapturing the Intimacy & Ecstasy in Your Relationship with God*

"Rabbi Elie Spitz's book is earnest, studied, brave, and honest. He treats the urgent topic of despair with directness, compassion, and a searching eye for wisdom."

—**Joshua Wolf Shenk**, director of The Rose O'Neill Literary House, Washington College; author of *Lincoln's Melancholy*

"Individuals who struggle will find comfort in these pages, as they link their own suffering to the suffering in the larger story of Jewish history and their healing to the resilience of the Jewish people. Elie Spitz is both courageous and generous in sharing his story. He is a powerful and compassionate role model for those in the midst of despair. Blessings to him and to those whose journey brings them to his words."

—**Rabbi Anne Brener**, author of *Mourning & Mitzvah: Walking the Mourner's Path through Grief to Healing*

"Opens the riches of Jewish wisdom to people of all faiths. [May help readers] depart from the narrowness of their suffering and recover the divine spark in their own lives. Read this book, and learn how your suffering may become a blessing to others."

—**Gordon Peerman**, Episcopal priest; psychotherapist; author of *Blessed Relief: What Christians Can Learn from Buddhists about Suffering*

"*Healing from Despair* is a profound book that offers a vocabulary to the confusing and alienating state of hopeless- ness. With words, stories and images, Spitz manages to describe what is often indescribable and offer comfort and hope as well as practical advice. I felt drawn into its pages and inspired by its wisdom."

—**Rabbi Karyn D. Kedar**, author of *The Bridge to Forgiveness: Stories and Prayers for Finding God and Restoring Wholeness*

Healing

from

Despair

Choosing Wholeness
in a Broken World

Rabbi Elie Kaplan Spitz
with Erica Shapiro Taylor
Foreword by Abraham J. Twerski, MD

For People of All Faiths, All Backgrounds
JEWISH LIGHTS Publishing
Woodstock, Vermont
www.jewishlights.com

Healing from Despair:
Choosing Wholeness in a Broken World

2008 Hardcover Edition, First Printing
©2008 by Elie Kaplan Spitz

All rights reserved. No part of this book may be reproduced or transmitted in any form or by any means, electronic or mechanical, including photo-copying, recording, or by any information storage and retrieval system, without permission in writing from the publisher.

For information regarding permission to reprint material from this book, please mail or fax your request in writing to Jewish Lights Publishing, Permissions Department, at the address / fax number listed at the bottom of this page, or e-mail your request to permissions@jewishlights.com.

Library of Congress Cataloging-in-Publication Data
Spitz, Elie Kaplan, 1954–
Healing from despair: choosing wholeness in a broken world / Elie Kaplan Spitz ; with Erica Shapiro Taylor ; foreword by Abraham J. Twerski.
p. cm.
"For people of all faiths, all backgrounds."
Includes bibliographical references.
ISBN-13: 978-1-58023-360-6 (hardcover)
ISBN-10: 1-58023-360-0 (hardcover)
1. Despair—Religious aspects—Judaism. 2. Suffering—Religious aspects—Judaism. 3. Depression, Mental—Religious aspects—Judaism. 4. Suicide—Religious aspects—Judaism. 5. Consolation (Judaism) 6. Healing—Religious aspects—Judaism. 7. Spitz, Elie Kaplan, 1954– I. Taylor, Erica Shapiro. II. Title.
BM645.S9S65 2008
296.7—dc22
2008028933

10 9 8 7 6 5 4 3 2 1

Manufactured in the United States of America
✿ Printed on recycled paper.
Jacket Design: Tim Holtz

For People of All Faiths, All Backgrounds
Published by Jewish Lights Publishing
A Division of LongHill Partners, Inc.
Sunset Farm Offices, Route 4, P.O. Box 237
Woodstock, VT 05091
Tel: (802) 457-4000 Fax: (802) 457-4004
www.jewishlights.com

With gratitude to the members of Congregation B'nai Israel, Tustin, California, who for over twenty years have been my teachers, friends, and flock. You have allowed me to grow as a rabbi and as a person.

—EKS

For my father, *zichrono levracha,* with love.

—EST

Contents

Foreword

In forty-five years of psychiatric practice, I have treated various emotional illnesses, among them, depressive disorders. Psychiatric textbooks list the more common symptoms of depression. Strangely, they do not adequately describe and explain a very frequent symptom of depression, one that many depressed patients do not volunteer, and one about which many therapists hesitate to ask—the despair due to a feeling of utter uselessness.

This relative paucity of discussion about the despair resulting from the feeling of utter uselessness may strike so sensitive a nerve in mental health professionals that they avoid the subject. Yet, it is this feeling that may cause the greatest distress for the depressed person, and may even lead to suicide. The despair of feeling utterly useless goes beyond pain, resulting in a total numbness. The absence of all feeling puts one's very existence into question. A person in despair may feel that there is no place for him or her on the planet Earth. A person who feels utterly useless and sees no possibility of one's existence ever having any meaning may find no reason to live.

If all Rabbi Elie Spitz had done with this book, *Healing from Despair: Choosing Wholeness in a Broken World*, was to provide a vivid description of despair, based on his personal travail, it would have been a major contribution. It would have enabled health professionals to investigate this "feeling of non-feeling" with their clients, and would have validated the feelings of patients in the depth of depression who believe that nobody could possibly understand their agony. But Rabbi Spitz goes further and, drawing on his own experience, shows that the awesome sense of despair and of feeling utterly useless can actually be the seed from which a sense of purpose and meaning, indeed a sense of mission, can sprout.

The wisest words in all my psychiatric training came from a peer early in the first year. I was discussing a patient with him, when he interrupted me and said, "Twerski, stop talking logic." I had to realize that my patient's problem was emotional, and logic does not apply to emotions.

What kind of human communication can help a person in distress? *Empathy*, the feeling that there is someone who can identify with another person's suffering. Emotions are very private, and cannot be described adequately in words. A person in emotional distress feels terribly alone. Empathy is a non-verbal sharing of feeling, so that one no longer feels the loneliness.

In the writings of the psychiatrist Frieda Fromm-Reichman, she noted that there was a glaring dearth of material in the psychiatric literature on loneliness. Dr. Fromm-Reichman postulated that loneliness is so anxiety provoking to mental health professionals that they veer away from this topic.

Conveying feelings via words is most difficult, yet Rabbi Elie Spitz has managed to do this, and someone in need of empathy can find it in *Healing from Despair: Choosing Wholeness in a Broken World.*

Rabbi Spitz points out that everything in existence must have a spark of divinity, and that that spark is of significance in the world. Awareness of that spark within oneself can banish the thick darkness that envelops the depressed individual and it can be the beginning of healing.

The Talmud says that Moses asked God why there is suffering, and God answered that as long as a person inhabits a physical body, he cannot possibly understand this. Following the revelation at Sinai, the Torah says, "Moses approached the thick cloud where God was." One might think that God's immanent presence would be in brightness, but Moses knew better. It is in the darkness of life that we may find God. Rabbi Spitz shows us how we can find hope, compassion, humility, gratitude, and the capacity to become a blessing in the darkness of despair. Yes, God may be found in the thickness of the cloud.

The loneliness of suffering is accentuated by the feeling that one has been abandoned by God. Rebbe Nachman of Breslov says that when he was in the depth of depression, he focused on the verse in Psalms (139:8), "If I ascend to heaven, You are there; if I make my bed in the lowest depths, behold, You are there." Rebbe Nachman said, "Indeed, I felt I was in Hell, but God was there with me. I was not alone."

A very spiritual person said, "God, when I am alone, there is nothing I can do, but when You are with me, there is nothing I *cannot* do." God may communicate directly to a human being, as God did to the prophets, or God may communicate with us via people. Rabbi Spitz's book is an embodiment of the psalmist's words, "God is close to the brokenhearted, and those crushed in spirit, God saves" (Ps. 34:19).

—ABRAHAM J. TWERSKI, MD

Acknowledgments

My beloved teacher Rabbi Simon Greenberg said, "When people ask how long your sermon took to prepare, tell them your age." Just as each sermon emerges from a lifetime of experience, so does this book. It took me many years to grow comfortable with my emotional traumas, to use my experience in my own work, and to formulate the lessons that I derived. In honor of turning fifty, I wrote up my account of my hospitalizations as my "first book." A year later, a dear friend committed suicide. I began to read widely on suicide, depression, and happiness (the antidote to all the painful material). During a year of writing, I composed a "second book" in a question-and-answer format, integrating my own story.

When I showed it to my friend and gifted editor, Erica Taylor, she reported, "You are guarded in how you write about this painful material. When you speak you do so with openness and directness. I type quickly. You know what you want to say and I will be your audience. How many talks would it be? We could get the writing done in eight or nine sessions." Erica and I met in my office for close to eight or nine months, two or three times a week for two or three hours a session. With patience and care she listened and probed, allowing me to speak more personally, directly, and expansively. This "third book" could not have emerged without Erica's encouragement, skill, and dedication.

Once we completed the manuscript, we asked a group of diverse friends to read it. We also shared the text with health care providers to make sure our ideas were medically sound. The editing spanned many months with the care and wisdom of the following readers: Bradley Shavit Artson, Carl Bendroff, Shai Cherry, Ari Goldman, Matt Goodman, Salomon Gruenwald, Ellie Herman, Dana Hollander, Leslie Kaufman, Marla Kaufman, Daniel Lang, David Lazar, Ray Lederman, David Levinson, Lorraine McCarty, Howard Mirowitz, Annie O'Reilly, Peter Pitzele, Susan Pitzele, Jack Riemer, Linda Spitz, Mark Spitz, Michael Steingart, Marcia Tilchin, Arlene Turner, Abraham Twerski, David Wertschafter, Michael Wolf.

Three accomplished writers had even earlier encouraged me to turn my story into a book. Brad Artson was the first colleague with whom I shared my hospitalizations as if revealing an embarrassing secret. His enduring friendship gave me the confidence to tell my story to others. Ari Goldman and I sat at a cafe one evening years ago and discussed what I should write my next book about. "Go with what feels most real to you," he counseled. I replied that it was healing from despair. He said, "Then that's your topic." Last, Alan Lew reinforced Ari's recommendation. In Jewish law, a group of three constitutes a court. These three friends helped motivate me to move forward into the thicket of research and writing about despair.

This is also an opportunity to thank Linda and Phil Lader, organizers of Renaissance Weekends. These gatherings of conversation over New Year's weekend in Charleston have exposed me to accomplished personalities such as Art Buchwald, whose courage inspired me to tell my own story.

Jewish Lights Publishing is a blessing for me. After Stuart M. Matlins, the publisher, listened to my description of the topic, he offered his encouragement, and later, his outstanding team and his ongoing wise counsel. My content editor, Bryna Fischer, brought her keen mind and Jewish learning to the text, offering much helpful guidance. Her reading occurred during her husband's struggle with cancer, making the content of the book all the more real and personal for her. May the memory of Barry Fischer endure for Bryna and her family as a blessing. Emily Wichland, vice president of Editorial and Production, and Heidi White, assistant editor, brought attention to detail and offered many thoughtful recommendations.

I am grateful to Dr. Abraham Twerski for composing the foreword to this book, for his writings of guidance and inspiration, and for his friendship.

I thank my family—my wife, Linda, and our children, Joseph Ephraim, Jonathan Tamir, and Anna Rose Miriam. You each give my life purpose and joy.

I conclude with the traditional blessing, praising God for giving me life, sustaining me, and allowing me to reach this moment.

Introduction

In the Company of Heroes and Healers

I know about despair. I know about despair from the inside. More than twenty years ago I was committed as a patient at three mental hospitals to keep me safe from my suicidal yearnings. For more than a decade after I had been ordained as a rabbi, I did not share the depths of the darkness, the particulars of my story, with my congregants. Only gradually did I begin to reveal my secret past in the course of my counseling work. Eventually I found that because I had tasted the bitter darkness, the ashes in my mouth, I could return to that place to offer empathy, understanding, and hope to souls in pain.

This book began with the desire to understand the events of my past, which I had kept hidden for so long, even from myself. In anticipation of turning fifty, I interviewed my siblings and the psychiatrist who had treated me many years before. I wrote up the account and found a greater sense of wholeness that came with increased understanding and acceptance. Soon after, I began a forty-week sabbatical traveling with my wife and three children to seventeen countries. Upon my return I attended a seminar for rabbis where an old friend sat with me at lunch. Two months later he drove his car off a cliff. I was devastated by his apparent suicide. I read about depression and suicide, seeking both psychological understanding and spiritual guidance. Although I found many fine books by psychotherapists, I found little that offered a spiritual understanding of despair. By spirituality, I mean those aspects of our humanity that make us distinct from animals, encompassing the quest for meaning and the practices of religious tradition that evoke perspective, gratitude, and hope.[1]

When I counsel, as when I write these words, I bring my own firsthand knowledge of despair along with the collective memory of the Jewish people. I have learned that while we do not wish for pain, we all will encounter suffering over the course of our lives. I have learned that our world is at once broken and filled with divine sparks. I have learned that when we encounter pain, we find that through crisis we may gain wisdom and the capacity to become a blessing to others. I now understand why the pearl is a universal symbol of wisdom. The pearl, formed when an irritant such as a grain of sand rubs against the surrounding soft tissue of a living mollusk, refracts light with beauty. Our own struggles may create the inner beauty that comes from heightened awareness and a greater capacity for kindness.

In my own life, my experiences of excruciating pain have allowed me to become more compassionate and humble. My encounter with a place of utter darkness has become the source of my faith in the goodness of the world. My memory of great loneliness has allowed me to become more present for others. In the Jewish tradition, our foundational story contains just this transformation. We remember that we were once slaves in Egypt who God led out as a free people and retell the story annually as a family ritual. In the retelling, we acknowledge that life contains bitterness. We affirm that, as our lives today are blessed with freedom, we must work to allow others to live without oppression. Informed by our particular history of suffering, we are called to be a blessing to others.

From the stories of despair brought to me over the years, I have come to see that the misery of inner turmoil may become strangely comforting, a part of our identity, of who we are in the world. And yet, the truth is that although suffering is an inevitable part of the human condition, even in the face of such suffering we have the power to choose. Although we may not be aware of it, we actually choose whether to hear messages of hope brought to us; we choose whether to identify as a person mired in despair or as a person daring to hope; we choose whether to focus on the bleakness or to see the goodness that is ever present in the world. Ultimately we choose whether to draw on our understanding of suffering to become a blessing to others. We come to see that despair is as timeless as humanity and as universal as this broken and beautiful world. In our times of despair, even those that beckon us toward death, we are truly in the company of heroes and healers of all religious faiths from every corner of the globe. Their stories come to us from long-ago Bible tales, historical documents, and present-day scholars.

I grew up in a safe, comfortable, middle-class world set in 1960s suburban America. And yet, even within my cozy childhood, I was always aware of my parents' wounds as Holocaust survivors. For my father, the war years spent in Hungarian forced labor camps were pushed deep within his memory. For my mother, memories of her youth scarred by the horrors of the Auschwitz concentration camp and forced labor were woven into my bedtime stories. I was aware as a child that suffering is as much a part of life as the warmth and calm of my family home.

I begin this book with a description of my upbringing to offer context for where I come from and for my descent into despair. My teacher Rabbi Wolfe Kelman said that there is no greater influence on a child than the unfulfilled dreams of a parent. Steve Martin, the comedian and author, illustrates this idea in his memoir, *Born Standing Up.*[2] When he was a young man, he perceived his father as distant and unsupportive, critical of him as a budding comedian. His father had yearned to be in show business but had only achieved bit parts in small theaters and instead sold real estate to earn a living.[3] When his father was dying, Steve returned to his childhood home in Orange County, California. He writes of standing at the foot of his father's bed:

> Ultimately we choose whether to draw on our understanding of suffering to become a blessing to others.

> There was another lengthy silence as we looked into each other's eyes. At last he said, "You did everything I wanted to do."
>
> "I did it for you," I said. Then we wept for the lost years. I was glad I didn't say the more complicated truth: "I did it *because* of you."[4]

In my case, I had very supportive parents. Yet, their traumas and yearnings would influence me profoundly in unconscious and unanticipated ways.

When I was a child, my mother told us stories of when she was a little girl, stories filled with the wonder and adventure of life in a town that stood at the crossroads of eastern Europe. My mother and father, Heddy and Arthur, each spoke six languages, a reflection of the diversity of peoples passing through their hometown of Munkacs, Czechoslovakia. My mother remembered the years from before the war as a time of warmth and joy. She attended a public school and was aware of the blossoming of democracy in her country. Her parents ran an inn and grocer's shop that gave the family some security and offered her father the freedom to dedicate himself to community and Torah study. She described to us her family's Shabbat table as a weekly celebration of the day of rest with festive meals, songs, and family. In her town the population was nearly half Jewish, and most of the Jews were religiously observant. In Munkacs my mother grew up with families supporting each other in times of need and celebrating together on occasions of happiness.

My mother sang to us. And the song that touched me most deeply was sung with both joy and sorrow in her voice. The lullaby "Home Again in Israel" spoke of our people's wanderings throughout nearly two thousand years of exile. The lullaby spoke of return to the Land of Israel. I knew that her tears were tears of joy for the dream fulfilled, the creation of the State of Israel in 1948. And I knew that she wept as well for the loss of family members and her childhood world.

For the Jew who had spent the war years hiding in barns, imprisoned in concentration camps, or fleeing through forests, the creation of the State of Israel represented a rebirth of a people. For nearly two thousand years, from the destruction of the Second Temple in 70 CE,[5] Jews were largely guests of other countries.[6] To study the history of the Jewish people is to understand the relationship of the Jewish people to despair and hope. Rodger Kamenetz writes in *The Jew in the Lotus*: "Jews have survived twenty centuries of exile and dispersion, persecution and vilification, economic hardship, expulsion, forced conversion, Crusades, Inquisition, blood libel, pogroms—you name it, Jews survived it."[7] The centuries of exile created a longing for stability, for a homeland. Through two thousand years Jews held fast to the promise that they would return to their homeland with the coming of the Messiah. In the shadow of destruction of the Temple by the Roman armies, Jewish prayer focused on the yearning for the Messianic era. The hope of return was at the core of Jewish identity: a hope that allowed Jews to survive oppression, persecution, and utter despair.

In my own childhood, I lived with a constant awareness of my parents' experience of being uprooted from their childhood homes and towns and memories. During the war years, my mother's parents, sister, and niece were murdered. Her brother died due to the brutal conditions. My father lost his brother and sister. The names of those killed were passed down to my generation as a way of honoring their lives and preserving their memories. My grandfather Marcus, celebrated in our family tales for dancing at weddings in order to raise funds for the dowries of poor brides, was murdered at the Bergen-Belsen concentration camp just weeks before the American army liberated the prisoners. My older brother, Mark, carries on his name, as well as his Hebrew name, *Mordechai Shmuel*, as do three of my cousins.[8] With the passing of the name from generation to generation, our family remembers his deeds of lovingkindness, and his memory becomes a blessing.

As a child, I heard stories not only of my mother's idyllic childhood in her hometown but also of the horrors of the concentration camps. She spoke of the separation from her family, from her home, and from her childhood sweetheart, my father. My mother described inmates of the death camps who lost all hope and threw themselves against the electrified barbed wire. After six months in Auschwitz, with the arrival of winter in 1944, my mother and three of her sisters were assigned to a forced labor group. Escorted by armed guards, they headed off into the countryside to dig anti-tank holes. The clothes she wore were too thin for the cold winds, and her shoes, given from a pile, were too large. For months they labored with little food. If a young woman was unable to work, she was shot as useless. When the snows began to fall, my mother's feet began to freeze. Hiding her pain and physical difficulties, she persisted. Yet each day her pain grew.

One night the group found shelter in a large barn. My mother told her sisters, "I cannot continue. I can barely stand, let alone walk on my swollen legs. I will stay hidden tonight in the straw. Escape is my only hope." Her sisters would not leave her. They each burrowed deep in the straw, using long hollow reeds to breathe. In the morning, they heard the soldiers bark out the familiar command to line up outside for the morning count. Soon, German soldiers were back in the barn screaming, "Stop hiding and get out immediately." Moments later, they heard one soldier say to another, "Look, there is an opening here in the boards. The women must have run away." They held their breath until the search ended. They remained buried in the straw throughout the day and the following night. As sunrise approached, a farmer entered the barn. He called out in Polish, "Another group will stay here tonight. If you are hiding, leave now." They never knew why he issued this warning. They waited a bit longer and then dashed toward the woods.

My mother's older sister, Shari, had a bit of good fortune. When she removed a loose heel from her shoe, she found a gold coin. As the sisters approached a nearby village, they spotted a young man driving cows along the road. They explained to him in Polish that they were Russians whose homes had been destroyed. Seeking work and a place to stay, Shari handed him the coin and asked for his help. The cow herder found each of them work and shelter in the village where they remained until the Russians arrived several months later. Liberated, they returned to their hometown to see who had survived.

I tell this story of pain and liberation as I remember my mother telling it. I also include in the endnotes a selection from my mother's diary, a recollection set down in honor of her sixtieth birthday.[9] When I was young, I did not consider the ways in which my mother's tales had become my own. Only much later would I realize how the harrowing imagery and the daring escape played out in my own life.

My parents' legacy left me in a bind. On the one hand, throughout my childhood, both my parents focused on the present and the future without dwelling on the past. Their ability to choose life despite all they had endured gave me great strength. They worked hard, they raised children who knew their love, and they supported their community as an expression of gratitude and with a sense of responsibility. I knew that my parents were different—they spoke English with an accent and they did not know the rules of baseball. I knew of my parents' wartime losses and of their gratitude for the freedom of America and for a safe national home in the Land of Israel. They instilled in me a profound desire to discover my gifts and to use them on behalf of others. On the other hand, my parents never processed the unfathomable suffering of the war years in order to come to terms with their profound loss. In my mother's last years, outrage and paranoia escaped from the corner of her soul where she had kept them tucked away for so long. Children do carry within them the wounds of their family's past. Some children are more sensitive to that pain than others. In looking back over my path, I can see that my parents' pain and my need to find a calling were factors that contributed to my own crisis as a young man. And yet, in time I found that the very responsibilities and burdens that brought me to the point of collapse ultimately became the very foundation of my identity and emerging strength and confidence.

Over the past twenty-five years, since the time I began my studies to be ordained as a rabbi, I have counseled some two thousand people. I have heard stories from the dark recesses of the human condition: death, the loss of a loved one; illness, the loss of capacity; divorce, the loss of love; betrayal, the loss of trust; infertility, the loss of a dream; addiction, the loss of free will; violence, the loss of security; deportation, the loss of home. With each loss comes a search for identity and purpose. When that search brings overwhelming pain we may engage in harmful behaviors. I have listened as deep secrets are revealed, and I have seen how when each story is shared, so is the weight of the shame and anguish it carries. I have counseled in mental institutions, in prisons, in rehabilitation hospitals, in hospice settings, at deathbeds, and at graveside. From a young man who was crushed by my responsibility to do meaningful work, I have become an older man who finds purpose in the responsibility of listening to stories of suffering.

To listen caringly is a privilege that may take a toll on the listener. To listen is to hear a story without giving in to the urge to solve the crisis, to give advice, to challenge false assumptions, or to fix the brokenness. Listening requires offering the gifts of time, patience, and kindness. The demands of active listening are illustrated in a story that I heard from Dr. Abraham Twerski, a contemporary psychiatrist and a Hasidic rabbi. In this story Rabbi David of Talna, a Hasidic master of nineteenth-century Europe, would counsel visitors all morning until at noontime his *shammas*, his secretary, would find him soaked in sweat. One day, finding him in this condition, his *shammas* asked, "Are you well, rabbi?" to which the rabbi replied, "I am fine, just tired. You see, when

> From a young man who was crushed by my responsibility to do meaningful work, I have become an older man who finds purpose in the responsibility of listening to stories of suffering.

someone comes to talk with me, I have to take my clothes off and put his clothes on in order to put myself in his place. But the reason the person comes to me is to hear the perspective of a rabbi. So I take off my visitor's clothes and put my own clothes back on. After a morning of repeated wardrobe changes, I am in need of a change of clothes myself."

My own encounter with despair became the crisis through which I found my capacity for empathy and for listening. Today, when a person brings me a story of despair, I am aware that each one of us is capable of spiraling into darkness, of undergoing the emotional unraveling that leads to chaos. I understand that we cannot explain our emotions with our intellect, nor can we perceive what we intuit using our five senses. I honor the gifts and the dignity that we each possess, even in our most painful moments. I believe that although from amid deep despair we cannot imagine our place and purpose, that our identity, worldview, and calling will be revealed with time. I know that the willingness to listen, to be present for a story of pain, sends a powerful message to the soul in despair: Even in this broken world, the kindness of a single heart reminds us to see the world as good, to search and discover the divine sparks embedded in creation and in ourselves.

> Even in this broken world, the kindness of a single heart reminds us to see the world as good.

As a rabbi, I can offer the wisdom that comes from beyond my own immediate experience and draws on biblical tales and the conversations of the sages. Their words come to us from across the centuries, spanning the time from the Bible through the Middle Ages to our day, and from around the globe, from Israel to Poland to Spain to Egypt. I can share the profound insight of the mystic sage Rebbe Nachman of Breslov, great grandson of Rabbi Israel Baal

Shem Tov, founder of the Hasidic movement: "All the world is a very narrow bridge." From despair, the place Rebbe Nachman called "bitter darkness,"[10] we see the world as narrow, unstable, terrifying. And yet, Rebbe Nachman continues, "The main thing, the principle thing, is not to be afraid." We learn that our work is to continue on, countering fear with hope, recognizing goodness despite brokenness. My beloved teacher Rabbi Simon Greenberg taught, "Our challenge in life is to see the world through God's eyes, as God in creation surveyed each day and pronounced: 'It is good.'" In a good but imperfect world, our calling is to participate in the work of healing the brokenness of the world even as we heal from our own loss and sorrow.

Hebrew scriptures, the foundation of collective Jewish memory, contain many ancient stories of souls in despair. The Torah acknowledges that to be alive in this world is to experience both joy and pain.[11] Yet the Torah—the books of Genesis, Exodus, Leviticus, Numbers, and Deuteronomy—rarely describes the thoughts and emotions of the biblical characters. The text generally presents only events, the plot as it occurs. Consider the chapters that tell of Moses wandering in the desert for years, his suffering becoming unbearable at times. Moses has taken on the responsibility for shepherding the Israelites from slavery in Egypt, through the desert, to freedom in the Promised Land. Torah scholars for generations have read the exodus from Egypt, literally "the narrow place," both as national history and as an allegory for liberation from slavery within the individual soul. The Israelites blame Moses for their hardships, complaining only days after departing from Egypt: "Were there no graves in Egypt that you took us to die in the wilderness? What is this that you have done to us to take us out of Egypt?" (Exod. 14:11).

Moses, remembered as a model of leadership, finally reaches a critical moment of crisis. He acknowledges that the Israelites, with their continued yearning for Egypt and their idealized memory of slavery, have worn him down. He cries out to God: "I alone cannot carry this entire nation, for it is too heavy for me! And if this is how you deal with me, then kill me now" (Num. 11:14). Moses is overcome by the people's insatiable cravings, by their hopelessness and his own, by the crushing weight of responsibility, and by his lack of strength for the role. The leader of a vast people, unable to meet its needs or allay its fears, he finds he is no longer capable of carrying out the tasks given to him by God. When we are in despair, we feel as Moses did at that point of exhaustion, filled with anger at life and at God, overwhelmed by fear that we can no longer carry the unbearable burdens of responsibility and pain, unsure if our lives have a worthy purpose. As we shall see, Moses heeds God's message of hope, which allows him to see the world as good, and to reclaim his purpose as a leader. Moses becomes a model for our own response to crisis.

We find another model for countering despair with choices in the Book of Genesis. Rachel is a woman who yearns for a child, pleading with her husband, Jacob, "Give me children—otherwise let me die"[12] (Gen. 30:1). After waiting seven years to marry Jacob—years marked by betrayal and disappointment—she is unable to conceive, even as her sister Leah delivers four sons. And yet Rachel does not allow her tragedy to define her, but instead considers an alternative course. She becomes a mother of children through a surrogate, her maid Bilhah. One lesson of the Rachel story is that even in times of despair, we can choose other paths rather than give up hope.

Our despair may come from a crisis of the moment or from pain that has persisted over time. We will see chronic suffering illustrated in the lives of leaders from Rebbe Nachman of Breslov, the Hasidic master of Ukraine, to

Abraham Lincoln, the American president throughout the Civil War. Our darkened path may not reveal our destination until we have traveled far away from the time of suffering. From the perspective of hindsight we may discern that out of the darkness, we have drawn light that has allowed us to lead and live more fully. Although we cannot foresee how we will one day emerge from despair and find our purpose revealed, our faith in the world's goodness allows us to accept that the crisis will pass or our burdens will become lighter. In the meanwhile, we have the power to choose to move toward healing. When we fail to hear messages of hope, to craft our evolving identity, or to see goodness in the world, despair will define us. When we choose to heed the messages, to assert a new identity, and to acknowledge the goodness present in creation, we move toward purpose.

Returning to the story of Rachel, we are reminded of the paradox of childbirth: the most excruciating pain that most women will know in their lifetimes comes from the contractions of labor and delivery. When Rachel dies in giving birth to her second son, Benjamin, we are made aware that the day a woman delivers a child is often the most dangerous time in her life. And yet women willingly choose to undergo childbirth and do so repeatedly. Rachel's story teaches that how we experience pain is largely a product of interpretation. The pain of giving birth is distinct from suffering because we see the pain as a necessary and natural part of bringing a new life into the world. Once the contractions abate, the suffering is transformed into a blessing, into gratitude for a new life. How we choose to interpret

> Our darkened path may not reveal our destination until we have traveled far away from the time of suffering.

even traumatic experiences will shape how we see the world. Our own suffering can become a blessing, which leads us to Job.

Job suffered at each of the levels on which we live our lives: physical and emotional, intellectual and spiritual. God grants Satan permission to test Job. In a single day Job loses his livestock, his flocks and shepherds, and his beloved children. Long-suffering Job at last reaches his limit, concluding that there is no justice in the world. God responds to Job's cries by speaking of the miracle of creation and the limits of humans. Through God's words, a bridge from the divine to the human, Job finds that he has been heard. He comes to realize that he will choose whether to listen to God's message, to forge his identity, and to form his worldview. With God's words, Job finds that he is not alone, that order and beauty are present amid the chaos in the world, even though loss and suffering will continue to be a part of life. Job models for us how conversation with God, whether manifest as prayer or as a still, small voice from within, establishes our relationship with a power greater than ourselves. Here is Job, a mere mortal, who merits being addressed by none other than God, the Creator.

> How we experience pain is largely a product of interpretation.

These ancient heroes and healers from the Bible offer us comfort by demonstrating that despair is ancient and eternal. Although the causes of our struggles may vary widely, the sense of darkness, chaos, and loneliness and the belief that suffering, injustice, and hopelessness prevail are common elements of despair. Ultimately these heroes and healers offer us hope: each one, when faced with great loss chose to accept a message of comfort, to seek purpose, and to see the world's goodness. The lessons of the past resonate with particular relevance in the aftermath of our own collapses. In my own case, I did not see the danger ahead. And like Job, I emerged with the blessings of humility and gratitude, with the capacity to see God's works as good.

What I hope to offer you is an understanding of the nature of despair, the awareness that even in our darkest moments we are blessed with the capacity and strength to heal, to change, and to find our purpose. We will explore how personal crisis has been a source of humility, gratitude, and strength for biblical characters like Rachel, Moses, and Job as well as modern figures like Churchill and Buber. We will trace the spiral through these next five chapters, downward from despair to depression to desperation, and upward to forgiving, healing, and on to blessings. Healing from despair is rarely a linear process. We may need to take a step back before we can move forward again. We would all wish to see—whether in ourselves or in our loved ones—healing that progresses every day. And yet the healing process is more of a slow, spiraling ascent than a straight line, tracing a course forward and then backward, following a rhythm unique to each soul.

In the chapters that follow you will find that characters, themes, and texts appear and reappear. My own story of despair, for example, is presented in pieces that follow the arc of the chapters. We will trace the downward spiral into despair and beyond, to the brink of the abyss. We will follow the upward spiral from the turning point to the place where firsthand knowledge of despair can be transformed into purpose. Although in an earlier version of this book I told my entire story from start to finish in a single chapter, in actuality our lives do not unfold in simple, discrete chapters with titles like "Education," "Love," and "Work." Our lives are not lived in an orderly sequence, presented like a resume. I think of our lives, and this book, as a tapestry. A hanging tapestry offers a coherent image to the viewer yet is actually composed of thousands of threads woven in and out and knotted, which are visible only on the reverse side, the side hidden from view. In this book the messiness of the meandering threads and concluding knots is presented for your consideration. We will pause to consider in each chapter the lessons of the stories offered.

Since the creation of humankind, despair has been an element of the human condition, a part of being alive. In encountering despair and seeking comfort, you may turn to your religious faith, you may lose faith and reject God outright, you may find yourself struggling to maintain faith, or you may encounter a creator who is the source of the divine spark in each human being. In striving to find meaning in the midst of pain, you may practice your religion with rituals and observances or you may choose instead to focus on the spiritual qualities that underlie religious practice, or both. Your approach to suffering may come from your experience as a student of text or of the human condition.

With this book, I hope to offer you comfort, a way of seeing despair that allows for hope, healing, and the blessing of performing deeds of kindness. When we become mired in anger and fear, we lose our capacity to understand the blessings of despair. And yet with time and willingness—because change is hard, even when change brings healing—we can reach a place from which we forgive ourselves, we heal from our wounds, and we find that the world is good. This book also offers tools for the soul, in the form of exercises and suggestions of practical guidance at the end of each chapter.

Before we look to the Jewish tradition's description of creation as broken and what that means for our own lives, let me share a prayer. When I teach on Shabbat mornings in our synagogue, I usually conclude with words to God. The prayer allows me, speaking on behalf of the congregation, to sum up and to craft a message:

> *Rebono shel ha'olam*, source of compassion and mystery, may it be Your will that out of the darkness of despair we kindle hope and healing that enable us to recognize that we are bearers of light, vessels of Your presence. Amen.

Tools for Perspective

Writing a Love Letter to Your Family

As a means of identifying your core values, compose a letter to your loved ones describing your life, the lessons that you have learned about what really matters, and your hopes for them. Such a letter can be a form of blessing, traditionally known as an ethical will and often presented to family after a person has passed.[13] Writing such a letter offers insight into how you see your own life at this moment, and it serves as a reminder of what you see as your purpose on this earth.

Reflections

Set aside thirty minutes to write a journal entry in response to one or more of these questions:

- What are some of the traumas or dreams of your parents that have shaped you?
- What has been your parents' influence on you, as sources of both weakness and strength?
- What dreams or traumas of your own do you see making an impact on those who are closest to you?

One

A Shattered Vessel

R abbi Isaac Luria, the sixteenth-century Torah scholar and mystic of Safed, Israel, left us with an enduring vision of creation.[1] The Lurianic view embraces the totality of creation: from the brokenness of the world to the divine light that permeates the world. Luria taught that before creation began, the Infinite One, *Ein Sof*, filled all that existed. Before God began creation, God withdrew, contracting to leave a vacuum of space to serve as the location of creation. This withdrawal is called *tzimtzum*, a Hebrew term that is translated in the context of Luria's writings as "self-contraction." Into the vacuum, the Infinite One shined a ray of divine light, an emanation of divine being. The vessels crafted to receive that light could not contain the intense power and shattered. Most of the light returned to its source, to *Ein Sof*. Left behind were shards from the broken vessels and lost bits of divine light. Those divine sparks remain present in every material manifestation of the creation.

Repairing a Broken World with Sacred Acts: Rabbi Luria's Worldview

Jewish mysticism, the striving to encounter the presence of God and to understand God's mystery, dates to the time of the earliest Jewish sacred texts. Mysticism became more widely studied with the acceptance of the Zohar, an allegorical commentary on Hebrew scripture that first appeared in manuscript form at the end of the thirteenth century and was printed in the sixteenth century. Rabbi Luria, a teacher of the Zohar, expanded on the Zohar's portrayal of creation. In Luria's description, our world is filled with contradictions: God is present but must withdraw prior to initiating creation; vessels purposely created to contain the divine light are shattered by the light's force; creation and chaos coexist. In this world of paradox, if we find ourselves alone in darkness and brokenness, if we find ourselves shattered and lost, we can hold fast to the knowledge that our despair is an inevitable part of existence ever since God created the world.

From the moment of the initial act of creation, chaos ensues as vessels are shattered and divine sparks are scattered. And yet from the chaos arises beauty, as the divine sparks sustain every element of creation, from a rock to a plant to a child. This account of the creation of the world contains a radical concept. Human acts are needed to liberate holy sparks, freeing them from matter to reconnect with the divine source. And more, God depends on our human acts to assist in the work of collecting the sparks. The Luria creation story tells us that in the brokenness of the world we can discern our purpose. We are called on to do the work of healing the broken world. If our world were perfect, we would not be obligated to undertake its repair. But our world has never been perfect, not even from the very first moment, when time and space began.

The power of the Lurianic description of creation is not found in its scientific truth—although there are remarkable parallels to the modern big bang theory of creation[2]—but is found rather in its metaphorical depiction of our purpose in the world. We are called to gather the lost holy sparks by engaging in sacred acts of living. In the tradition, sacred acts not only involve our relationship to the Creator but include deeds of kindness offered to others. This work of healing the brokenness is called *tikkun olam*, repair of the world.

For the mystics, deeds of goodness, including ritual acts, literally raised sparks to return to their source. Today, deeds of kindness are works of *tikkun olam*, from parents who honor a child's memory by supporting medical research to the person who listens with compassion and brings comfort to a friend in pain. We are

> God depends on our human acts to assist in the work of collecting the sparks.

at once broken into bits and yet are containers for sparks of divine light. Our shattered selves may find comfort in this truth: that in being shattered, we discover a deeper capacity to do the work of repair, and therein we find our calling, our purpose.

The causes of despair, depression, and even desperation are unique to each individual. And yet our individual stories of despair share a common bond. For each of us, the descent into darkness results from the convergence of a multitude of factors, like heavy burdens that weigh us down over the course of our lives as we take on the trials and tribulations that come with being alive. There are times when we can relate to the words of the psalmist: "For my wrongdoings are ... as an onerous burden; they are too heavy for me.... I am bent and bowed down greatly, all day in dark melancholy, I go" (Ps. 38:5, 7).

A Sickness of the Soul: My Story of Collapse

My own unraveling began with a physical illness. Only years after my return from the depths was I able to understand that my collapse was years in the making, within my body, my heart, my mind, and my soul. Even on the verge of my own spiral down, I had no sense of the immensity of the impending disaster. The trigger for my own decline was a physical illness, a case of viral encephalitis diagnosed when I was twenty-seven. Up until that moment in my life, I appeared healthy and strong. I had run the Boston Marathon and passed three state bar exams. I was the author of a legal brief presented to the U.S. Supreme Court on a matter of criminal procedure. I was working as legal counsel for the Brigham and Women's Hospital, a collective of Harvard teaching hospitals, and teaching Jewish Thought in a religious high school every Sunday. My collapse resulted from a sort of perfect storm, a colliding of factors physical, intellectual, emotional, and spiritual that I could not withstand.

One Sunday I visited the Brigham Hospital emergency room, suffering from exhaustion and a stiff neck. The emergency room doctor diagnosed meningitis and recommended several weeks of bed rest. One week later, despite the Boston winter, I returned to running and to work. Two weeks later, I was admitted to the hospital and diagnosed with encephalitis, a swelling of the brain lining that leads to a major disruption of brain chemistry. I have little recollection of my first few days in the hospital. A responsible son, a diligent student, a lawyer with a prestigious position, I saw all of my hopes and dreams slipping away in a morass of confused thought. What I do remember of my two-week hospital stay is calming myself by singing my mother's lullaby, "Home Again in Israel." One incident that my cousin Joe, a neurologist, told me about much later was my phone call to him from my hospital bed. I called in a state of panic to report: "Nazis are trying to shut me into a coffin." This episode from my delirium reveals the presence of my mother's sufferings in my own unconscious mind.

I also remember that during my hospitalization, a clinical professor from Harvard Medical School interviewed me before a group of medical school students to demonstrate how to evaluate a patient's mental status. The professor spoke to me with a condescension that the renowned twentieth century professor of Bible and theology scholar Martin Buber would describe as characteristic of an I-It relationship, one in which a person treats another as an object (more on this in chapter 5). I remember—even though I was not thinking clearly—how he failed to address me by name, treating me as if I were not present and demonstrating to the students a manner of complete disrespect for the patient. This experience has become a source I draw on in treating people with dignity at all times.

When I returned to work I was conscious that I was no longer whole, that I was in some sense broken, that I was forever altered. My ability to concentrate was impaired. Without focus or energy for my work, I would read the newspaper at my desk in the hospital's legal department. I found myself angry, filled with fear, and increasingly isolated. To those who offered companionship and care I responded with arrogance and impatience, too emotionally self-absorbed to maintain a relationship. Illness represents loss—at the most conscious level a loss of health and of the capacity to live a productive life, and at a deeper level a loss of trust that all is right with the world. Years later, a close friend told me how the illness had changed me from a kind and easygoing person to an arrogant fellow with an attitude of impatience. Aware that I could not work and profoundly uncertain of whether I was meant to be a lawyer, I sold all of my possessions—my car, my Persian rug, my stereo—with the idea of traveling to Tahiti. Tahiti for me represented a paradise found, a place of harmony. Perhaps in choosing to travel so far to an unknown locale, I was trying to flee my self. I had no clue that within a year I would have spiraled down into utter darkness, leading to a series of hospitalizations in mental hospitals, a story I will tell in greater detail in the next chapter.

The Weight of the Burdens We Bear: Stories from Scripture

Stories of the Bible broaden our understanding of the human condition and how collapse is often the product of accumulated weights. In reading these tales, we find that the experiences of our own lives are also present in our collective memory. Finding despair in the lives of our biblical heroes normalizes and adds context to our own life stories.

Let's turn again to the story of Rachel in the Bible. She and Jacob had fallen in love at first sight by a well. When Rachel's father, Laban, required seven years of service for Jacob to take her as a wife, the Bible tells us, "Jacob worked seven years for Rachel, but he loved her so much, it seemed like no more than a few days" (Gen. 29:20). In one of the many examples of dysfunctional family behavior that appear in Genesis, Jacob's future father-in-law switched the brides on the wedding night. In the morning, Jacob discovered that he had married Leah, Rachel's older sister. Although Jacob was permitted to marry Rachel after the week of wedding festivities for Leah, he had to pledge another seven years of labor to her father.

By the time Rachel declared, "Give me children or I shall die," she was already carrying tremendous burdens. Each burden represented a loss: the loss of trust in her father who had betrayed her by marrying off Leah to Jacob; the loss of a sibling bond in the rivalry with Leah for the love of Jacob; and the loss of hope to become a mother of children even as her sister gave birth to four sons. In response to Rachel's plea, the text records, "Jacob became furious with Rachel, 'Shall I take God's place?' he said; 'It is God who is holding back the fruit of your womb'" (Gen. 30:2).[3] Jacob's indignation is all the more perplexing in light of the precedent set when his own mother experienced infertility. His father, Isaac, "pleaded with God for her sake; God granted his plea, and Rebecca became pregnant" (Gen. 25:21). Jacob himself was a product of caring prayer! For Rachel, the cumulative disappointments of her past and the rebuke by her husband made the added weight of her inability to conceive unbearable.

Yet Rachel found her purpose from that shattered place and demonstrated resilience, endurance, and the ability to maintain the relationship with a husband who adored her. She eventually became the mother of two sons through her maid-servant Bilhah and of two more sons that she later conceived and delivered herself. In this broken world, Rachel would die in delivering her second son. In understanding the full weight of the burdens upon Rachel and her ability to move forward purposefully, we gain awareness that we are not alone with our limitations as humans, beings who at times are no more or less than vessels shattered by divine emanations.

In the case of Moses, his crisis followed years of struggle. Soon after the people reached freedom and Moses began serving as the shepherd of the people, his father-in-law, Jethro, warned him about carrying burdens. Watching Moses stand from morning to night judging the people's cases, the older, experienced leader cautioned: "What you are doing is not good. You are going to wear yourself out along with this nation that is with you. Your responsibility is too great. You cannot do it all alone" (Exod. 18:17–18). Jethro advised Moses to appoint a hierarchy of judges so that he could decide only the major cases. To Moses's credit he followed the advice of his father-in-law.

The crisis Moses encountered later was much more serious. His very purpose as a leader and as a servant of God was called into question. For over two years, the people had received food in the form of heaven-sent dew, called manna. Although the manna was presented to the people, who had no need to plant or harvest in order to eat, they grumbled:

> "Who's going to give us some meat to eat? We fondly remember the fish that we could eat in Egypt at no cost, along with the cucumbers, melons, leeks, onions and garlic. But now our spirits are dried up, with nothing but the manna before our eyes." (Num. 11:4–6)

The people were stuck in a state of misery, unable to appreciate the glory of their freedom and their newfound purpose of living in covenant with God. They expressed their hopelessness by focusing on the trivial: onions and garlic.

Finally, Moses cried out in despair: "I alone cannot carry this entire nation, for it is too heavy for me! And if this is how you deal with me, then kill me now!" (Num. 11:14). Burdened with responsibilities, unappreciated by the Israelites, without a sense of purpose, Moses was overwhelmed. From a place of despair, we may feel like Moses in crisis, exhausted by the weight of our burdens, filled with anger at God that we have been made to suffer, and overwhelmed by fear that we can no longer bear the responsibility and pain. And at that moment, God had a message for Moses, instructing him to gather seventy

With purpose and hope we can see the world as good, even when our situation remains unchanged.

elders: "When I lower My essence and speak to you there, I will cause some of the spirit that you possess to emanate and I will grant it to them. You will then not have to bear the weight all alone" (Num. 11:17).

Moses gathered the seventy elders outside the camp, around his tent. God descended in a cloud and caused the spirit that had been placed on Moses to emanate upon the seventy, who spoke in ecstasy (Num. 11:25). God would also bring the people quail, but this unanticipated invitation by God quelled Moses's despair. Although the transfer of the divine spirit was only temporary, this event renewed his sense of mission. In seeing that there were others who shared a commitment to God and an appreciation for freedom, hope replaced a feeling of futility. God had also shown Moses that he served a unique role as a spiritual conduit for others. The lessons to be drawn from Moses's experiences are:

- Even the powerful and the strong are vulnerable to collapse and must share their burdens.
- Lack of purpose is a weighty burden. Moses's recognition that God needed him to lead the people and serve as a spiritual conduit gave him purpose. When others that we admire validate our commitments and goals, we can see beyond immediate complaints and challenges.
- From a place of hopelessness we may heed a caring message that moves us from crisis to hope. Moses heeded Jethro's counsel and accepted God's offer of help. It is often hard to ask for help when it is needed and to accept help when it is offered, yet doing so can give us renewed perspective.
- With purpose and hope we can see the world as good, even when our situation (such as Moses's responsibilities for a multitude or Rachel's infertility) remains unchanged.

Identifying with the Biblical Language of Despair

In the story of Moses, we see how the language of the Torah is crafted to convey the great weight of the burdens placed upon him. Born into a time in which his people were oppressed by slave masters, the grown Moses "went out to his brethren and observed their burdens" (Exod. 2:11). Later in the story, Moses protested that the Children of Israel would not listen to him, "for I am heavy of mouth and heavy of speech" (Exod. 4:10), repeating the word *heavy* to emphasize his inadequacy as a leader. And when Moses could bear no more, he told God: "I alone cannot carry this entire nation, for it is too heavy for me!" (Num. 11:14). Despair feels like a heavy, dark, impossible weight, caused by a multitude of burdens gathered over time, perhaps until a final single blow crushes us. From his low point, Moses went on to find his purpose in the work of leading the people, reconciling God to the Israelites, and calling upon God to be merciful (Num. 14:19).

The choice of words in scripture conveys that the weight of despair can feel confining. The Hebrew word for "trouble" is *tzar*, which means narrow. When we are weighed down by emotional distress we may feel confined to a narrow place, restricted to a rut. The word for "troubles"—*tzarot* in Hebrew, *tzures* in Yiddish—describes everything from petty aggravations to life crises. Burdens are a natural part of the world in which we are blessed to live. The word *tzarot* shares its three-letter root with *mitzrayim*, or Egypt, the place where we toiled as slaves carrying terrible burdens. Many rabbis throughout the ages have interpreted *mitzrayim* as the inner condition of feeling overwhelmed by burdens and have interpreted *mitzrayim* as the inner state of enslavement. The challenge, as expressed by Rabbi Israel of Kozhenitz in the 1700s, is that "Every person must become free from Egypt every day."[4] The task of carrying our burdens without succumbing to despair is ongoing.

The psalmists often chose the word *tzar* or a related word to express distress (see Psalms 25, 46, 69, 86). In Psalm 118 we find: "From the *maitzar* [the narrow place], I called to God." Thousands of years ago, those psalms, particularly those that are attributed to King David, emphasized that despair is a narrow, dark, desperate place. Although we are never entirely free of fears and sorrows, we may choose within this world of woes to see the world as good, even marvelous. The progression appears throughout the psalms—from distress to faith to hope. In reading psalms, we find comfort in the understanding that anguish and hope are part of life. At the end of this chapter, I recommend selected psalms that may offer comfort, insight, and celebration.

In the Book of Job, the word *tzar* is used repeatedly to describe Job's distress and anguish.[5] Job questions: Is there any meaning and purpose to life in light of suffering and injustice? He believes in a just God and lives his life with faithfulness to that God. When God allows Satan to bring suffering to Job, he responds faithfully: "Naked did I emerge from my mother's womb, and naked shall I return there. God has given, and God has taken away, blessed be the name of God" (Job 1:21–22). When God permits Satan to inflict physical pain upon Job, Job at last cries out, demanding, "Did I not weep for the heavily burdened, did I not sorrow for the destitute? I looked forward to good fortune, but evil came; I hoped for light, but darkness came.... Why then is this my portion from God above and the legacy of the Almighty on high?" (Job 30:25–26; 31:2).

God's response, regarding the mystery and miracle of creation, brings comfort to Job. Although he remains lost and alone in a brutal world of injustice and suffering, and although he cannot explain the pain he has suffered, he understands the choices open to him are to hear God's words, to forge his identity, and to form a worldview rooted in humility and gratitude. Job tells God, "I had heard of you through hearsay, but now my eye has beheld you, therefore I renounce my words and relent for I am but dust and ashes" (Job 42:6). We will see later that President Abraham Lincoln turned to the Book of Job repeatedly as a source of solace during the Civil War. Rereading these sacred texts allows us to perceive new insights and offers us comfort as we link our own experiences with those of the inspired sages and healers of the past.

When All Joy Is Gone: The Rambam's Crisis

Jewish study is a conversation across space and time. Young students are taught the saying: From Moses (the Moses of the Torah) to Moses (Rabbi Moshe ben Maimon of the twelfth century) there was none like Moses.[6] Let's move through history to consider the story of the illustrious scholar Rabbi Moshe ben Maimon, known also as Maimonides, or by his Hebrew initials as the Rambam. Maimonides suffered a complete collapse under the weight of his own burdens and yet ultimately transformed his despair into his life's work, a source of blessing to this day. Born in Cordoba in 1135, Maimonides lived in a troubled time when the Jews of Spain suffered under the ruling Almohades. When this Berber tribe governed Spain, they forced Jews—as well as Christians and dissident Muslims—to convert to Islam, emigrate, or face execution. The Jewish community, forced to pray in secrecy in their homes, faced a crisis of identity over whether to continue to utter prayers, which seemed to be unheard and without purpose, at risk of their lives. Into this broken world came Moshe, the son of a judge in the Jewish court.

The Rambam traced his lineage to Rabbi Yehuda HaNasi, renowned as the editor of the Mishnah. The Mishnah is the rabbinic law passed down through the generations orally until it was published in third-century Israel to become the foundation of later Jewish legal discourse. Maimonides' mother died in childbirth, leaving him to a scholarly and demanding father. Around 1157, when the Almohades burned the synagogues and houses of study to the ground, the family fled from Cordoba to Almeria, and when the Almohades captured Almeria, they fled again, arriving in Fez, Morocco. Maimonides was nearly killed for refusing to convert to Islam, but he was saved thanks to the intervention of a Muslim teacher. The family fled Fez, arriving in the Land of Israel in 1165. Later, Maimonides' family settled in old Cairo. In Egypt, Maimonides wrote that his sensitivity to suffering developed early in his life: "Since we went into exile, the persecutions have not stopped. I have known affliction since childhood, since the womb."[7] As a young man, the Rambam already bore the burdens of a lifetime: the loss of his mother, his father's high expectations, the flight from his home, and the persistent persecution of his community.

In his youth Maimonides studied many subjects in addition to Torah and its commentaries, including mathematics and natural sciences, astronomy and medicine, the theology of Islam and the philosophy of ancient Greece. At age twenty-three he began to write his influential commentary on the Mishnah. He described the challenge, undertaken amid physical danger: "The burden I assumed was by no means light.... My heart was afflicted by the miseries of the time, by the fate of exile that God has brought upon us."[8] Maimonides' next great work, the fourteen-volume *Mishneh Torah* (literally, a second Torah), was the first encyclopedia of Jewish law. In the *Mishneh Torah*, Maimonides drew on the teachings of thousands of earlier rabbis, as presented in the Talmud,[9] biblical commentaries, and the legal opinions up until his own day. In the forward to the *Mishneh Torah*, the Rambam wrote: "for if someone studies first the Torah and then this work, he will know all the teaching of oral tradition and will not have to consult any other work." Maimonides was able to devote ten years to composing a commentary to the Mishnah and twelve years to the *Mishneh Torah* with the support of his younger brother, David, a trader in precious stones. But in 1173 David's ship sank in the Indian Ocean on a voyage to India.

The Rambam, in mourning the loss of his beloved brother, spent a year in his bed in the depths of despair, and still the pain persisted. In his words:

> Years have waned, but I still mourn and find no solace.... My only joy was to see him. All my joy is gone. He has passed on to eternal life, leaving me shattered in a strange land. Whenever I see his handwriting or one of his books, my heart turns over in me, and my grief comes awake again.... If it were not for the Torah ... I would perish in my wretchedness.[10]

These words come to us after eight hundred years fresh with anguish. In later writing, Maimonides demonstrated his insight into the weight of great loss: "All thinking men are rendered perplexed and helpless by experiences like those of Job.... [O]ne may say that sometimes the blameless perfect man ... may be struck by heavy, unexpected, and uninterrupted evil."[11] Yet in time he learned from his own ordeal that "Man needs loving people all his life. One needs them in a time of affliction; in a time of physical weakness, one is dependent on their assistance."[12] The Rambam eventually emerged from his despair, as we shall see in chapter 4, with new purpose: partnering with God in healing the world and transforming his despair into the blessings of humility and gratitude.

All the World Is a Narrow Bridge: Rebbe Nachman's Despair

Centuries later, the Jews were still yearning to return to their homeland, still awaiting the coming of the Messiah. Rebbe Nachman of Breslov—the Hasidic master we met briefly in the Introduction—was born in 1772 in Ukraine into a time marked by persecution and poverty. Nachman was the great grandson of Rabbi Israel Ba'al Shem Tov, the founder of Hasidism, known by his Hebrew initials as the Besht. From an early age Rebbe Nachman was identified as the heir to his great grandfather's legacy. The biography of Rebbe Nachman prepared by his disciple, Rabbi Nathan of Nemirov, describes how this great responsibility became a burden to him early in life. Rabbi Nathan recounts a tale of six-year-old Nachman visiting the grave of his great grandfather on a cold winter's night to pray for release from evil thoughts. The story— whether historically accurate or not—illustrates the weighty expectations that Rebbe Nachman carried from his childhood.

In his youth Nachman experienced constant turmoil: Would God listen to him? Was he worthy to be a rabbi? Could he overcome his sexual longings and focus on study? Rabbi Nathan tells of the young Nachman: "He would often speak to God in heartfelt supplications and pleas. It seemed to him that he was being pushed away ... as though he were utterly unwanted.... At times he would become depressed.... Then he would catch himself and be overcome with shame for having called the goodness of God into question."[13] Rebbe Nachman was burdened with doubts that he could live a life worthy of a pious Jew, let alone as the leader of a movement that had reached thousands of eastern European Jews in times of despair. Like Moses, he accepted responsibility

for the spiritual well-being of an extended community, pro-
claiming himself the *tzaddik hador*, the righteous one of his
own generation, whose personal redemptive power could
raise the oppressed Jews of his community closer to the
Almighty. Rabbi Nathan draws a connection between Rebbe
Nachman and Moses, comparing Rebbe Nachman's travels
through the Ukrainian countryside of the eighteenth century to Moses and the Israelites' wanderings in ancient
times through the desert.[14]

In 1798 Rebbe Nachman sailed to the Holy Land. In his
biography *Tormented Master: The Life and Spiritual Quest of
Rabbi Nahman of Bratslav*, Professor Arthur Green[15] described
the burdens that afflicted Rabbi Nahman, also known as
Rebbe Nachman, in his lifetime. Nachman's life "was one of
constant struggle, of constant rise and fall in relationship to
God, a life alternating between periods of bleak depression
leading him to the brink of despair and redoubled efforts to
try to come close to God."[16] A sensitive child, burdened by his
natural physical desires and the emotional and intellectual
demands he inherited as the heir to the Ba'al Shem Tov, Rebbe
Nachman entered into depressed periods throughout his life.
After his arrival in Israel, observers reported of Nachman:
"Tremendous worry and broken heartedness were aroused in
him, he announced that he wanted to depart at once, without
visiting any of the other holy places."[17] Nachman had come to
Israel in search of greater peace but found his expectations
shattered: "Realizing as he did, a day after his arrival, that
the burdens which had always weighed upon his soul had
not been lifted from him as he set foot on the holy soil ... he
fell into a depression that troubled him until he left Haifa."[18]
Nachman's crisis in Israel became his turning point. From
the depths of despair, Nachman found purpose in serving his
community. He returned home to bring hope to the persecuted Jews as a leader of Hasidism in Ukraine.[19]

From Rebbe Nachman's own despair—"his temperament was so unstable, his sensitivity so acute, his intelligence so lively and precocious, that he experienced and received life like a wound"[20]—emerged an extraordinary source of hope and healing. His capacity to do the work of repair came from his experience as a shattered vessel in a broken world. Arthur Green writes, "Nahman is capable of lifting you out of despair and transforming your spiritual life not because of his great compassion from above, but rather because he has been through all of your torments, and worse, in his own life."[21] Nachman's refusal to succumb to despair reached even into the concentration camps. Elie Wiesel tells us: "But my first Hasid of Bratzlav, I met over there, in

> From despair may arise the calling to do the work of repair.

the kingdom of night. He repeated to anyone willing to listen the words of his Rebbe, the only Rebbe to survive himself: 'For the love of heaven, Jews, do not despair!' He prayed and told stories. I have forgotten his name. But not his voice."[22] Rebbe Nachman's life remained a source of hope for Jews long after his death.[23]

What do we learn from the biblical and historic figures who struggle with despair, who feel unworthy, who find God to be unjust? We learn that in our broken world—broken from the moment of creation—many of us will arrive at a time when, as shattered vessels, we experience despair as deep and dark, heavy and desperate. We learn that despair comes from the cumulative weight of burdens—losses, wounds, responsibilities, and questions of purpose. The responsibilities and losses that once crushed us to the ground beneath their weight may become our source of insight and clarity. From despair may arise the calling to do the work of repair.

The Four Levels of Loss: Physical, Emotional, Intellectual, and Spiritual

Looking back from the perspective of twenty-five years, I cannot pinpoint a single moment when all was lost. Neither can I identify a single cause of despair. Despair is a whirlwind, a spiraling downward that we enter at the point of a diagnosis, a crisis, or a tragedy, and the cumulative impact is greater than the total weight of the individual burdens we carry. The spiral creates a momentum, so that we find our thoughts racing toward gloom, and we can no longer sleep or eat or meet our needs. In my own case, the bout with encephalitis would seem to be the sole and single cause of my eventual fall into despair. However, in looking back I can identify burdens, like heavy stones, that I was carrying before the encephalitis struck. I can see that my own burdens included my unconscious responses to the wounds of my parents' past that neither they nor I had processed. I carried the weight of an exaggerated sense of obligation to give *nachas*, pride and joy, to my parents who had suffered so much. I believed I was meant to honor my family's past by finding a calling, a significant purpose.

We all carry burdens from our parents, whether the weight of high expectations or the anger of a bitter divorce, whether the anxiety of living in a world that is unpredictable or the responsibility of honoring them with deeds of goodness. With the onset of the encephalitis, my capacity to carry the weight of the past—which I had never before considered or examined—was severely compromised and the illness itself added yet another burden. In short, my strength to carry my psychological burdens had been diminished by the physical illness, while the weight of the burden had increased with my illness and my fear of failure to find my path.

In my counseling I draw on this experience of being shattered by a sickness in which physical, emotional, intellectual, and spiritual factors seemed to have converged and even conspired to bring about my fall. When I listen to the stories that are brought to me nearly every day, I am reminded that sacred Jewish text is traditionally approached on four levels.[24] For the rabbis who have studied and written commentaries on the Bible for centuries, the text contains multiple levels of meaning that can be uncovered and interpreted endlessly.[25]

Rabbi Zalman Schachter-Shalomi is a master teacher of Jewish mysticism who escaped from Europe under the Nazis to the United States where he became the founder of the Jewish Renewal Movement. In his writings, he identifies the levels of reading the Torah with the four nested worlds of creation described by the mystics: *pshat* (simple), meaning the basic facts perceived by the senses; *remez* (hint), meaning the underlying emotional message that can be felt; *drash* (derived), meaning the analytic intellectual reading; and *sod* (secret), meaning the mysterious level that can only be intuited.[26] The initial letters of the names of these four levels spell the Hebrew word *pardes*, an orchard or a paradise. Reb Zalman uses these four levels in his counseling, which has influenced my approach as well.[27]

When a person brings me a story of loss, I listen as if honoring a sacred text. On the *pshat* level, I listen to learn what happened: the simple events in chronological order, the characters, and the physical realities. Then comes the level of *remez*, the emotional responses, whether anger, guilt, or fear, that require a caring presence for the telling of the story. At the *drash* level the story is analyzed intellectually for issues that can be addressed, perhaps theologically or with the aid of a physician or a fellow survivor. And for *sod*, the mystical level, understanding must be intuitive, the listener must uncover the unspoken.

For example, a man comes to me in despair with a description of his cancer, a story that contains the four nested levels of loss. On the *pshat* level, the physical facts, he explains how he was diagnosed, the course of his treatment, the pain he has experienced, and the impact on his family members. On the *remez* level, the emotional expression, he shares his anger at God for cursing him with this illness, his fear of death, and his guilt over inflicting so much emotional pain on his family. On the *drash* level, the analytic, intellectual dimension, he may ask for guidance— a referral to a specialist in oncology, breathing techniques to address anxiety, a book on ethical wills for composing a letter of life's lessons for his family, or suggestions on how to make the best use of his time. At the *sod* level, the spiritual questions and their answers may be intuited. These issues may concern our purpose on this earth, the meaning of our lives, the legacy we leave our loved ones, and whether our souls survive.

For some people, peace comes only at the intuitive level of *sod*. At this level there are no simplistic answers, only a glimpse of enduring goodness that transcends our logical minds. I think of a story of heart-rending, shattering despair. An eighteen-year-old daughter, a prodigy, an only child who used her talents to inspire everyone around her, borrowed a friend's motorcycle on Passover eve. The motorcycle collided with a rock, and she died in the crash. Her father called me after reading my book *Does the Soul Survive? A Jewish Journey to Belief in Afterlife, Past Lives and Living with Purpose* (Jewish Lights).[28] What the father and mother found to be the most unbearable burden was the unrealized potential of their daughter's life—the loss of all she could have been, of her future great works and deeds. I could only say to the grieving parents that in this world there exist mystery and enduring goodness. This is the fourth level. We may describe on the physical level what happened, we may express on the emotional level the vast sorrow of the wound from a child's death, and we may understand on the intellectual level that bad things happen that we cannot explain, that the world operates according to its order. But at the spiritual, intuitive level, we may gain a fleeting, penetrating perception that the world contains divine sparks of goodness, that light and dark, order and chaos coexist.

On this level we may discover, as did Job, a faith that our lives matter to a presence who transcends our understanding. We may hold fast to simple truths, like the psalmist who proclaimed, "How great are Your works O' Lord, Your thoughts are infinitely profound" (Ps. 92:6). Given that God is the source of consciousness, the grand Creator, there may be a response beyond our comprehension. For Maimonides— the scholar of science and mathematics, theology and philosophy—the fourth level of intuition allows humankind to reach an understanding of the world and our lives: "With all his wisdom, his research and efforts, man has no other choice than to leave his business in the hands of the Creator, to pray to Him and beg Him to grant understanding, lead him to the right road, and reveal the mysteries to him."[29] We find the fourth level reflected in the words of Hannah Szenes, who fled Nazi-occupied Hungary for the safety of Palestine and then risked everything, returning to rescue Hungarian Jews in peril. Before she was captured and executed by the Nazis at age twenty-three, Hannah wrote a poem titled "*Yesh Kokhavim*," "There Are Stars":

There are stars whose light reaches the earth
only after they themselves have disintegrated and are
        no more ...
And there are people whose memory
lights the world after they have passed from it
These lights which shine in the darkest night
are those which illumine for us the path.

Hannah Szenes foretold her own tragic end and intuited that her purpose would outlast her short time on earth.

The Human Condition: Shattered Souls, Broken Backs

We find then that each story of despair has been caused by burdens on four levels, some of which may lie beyond our comprehension. How do we, shattered vessels in a broken world, bear the weight of our burdens and ultimately work to heal both ourselves and the world? I think of despairing souls, whether suffering from chronic despair that leaves them struggling to find peace or in shock after a trauma that makes the world seem out of balance, or both, using the analogy of the strength of the back. Each of us is born with certain characteristics. Our innate gifts determine to a large degree whether we are cheerful, optimistic, or adventurous. To understand the power of these innate traits in determining our personalities, we need only consider the differences between siblings raised in the same home. Life can develop our strengths or exacerbate our weaknesses. On the one hand, we may choose to be open to messages of hope, to form an identity of purpose, and to perceive the goodness in the world. On the other hand, when we experience our struggles as burdens, identifying as victims in a world of sorrow, we compromise the capacity of our spirits to bear weight.

Over our lifetimes, we pile burdens upon our backs, our spirits. These weights represent losses—whether through love lost, children's suffering, lack of purpose, expectations unmet, illness, or death. For Rachel of the Torah, the burdens were betrayal by her father, a husband who failed to offer comfort, a broken relationship with her sister, and the disappointment of her infertility. For Moses, leader of the people, the burdens included separation at birth from his family, the oppression of his people, God's expectations of him as a leader, and the ingratitude of the Israelites in the desert. For Maimonides, the burdens were the loss of his mother, the great expectations of his lineage, constant persecution, the pressures of scholarship, and the death of his brother. And for Rebbe Nachman the burden was inheritance of a great legacy thrust upon a sensitive soul. For me, my spirit was weakened by meningitis and encephalitis, but I already carried burdens—how to realize my parents' dreams, how to make my life purposeful—that had compromised my strength before I became ill. Because I had not learned to understand those burdens, I found I could not bear the additional weight from the illness.

When we experience loss, the injury may leave us more compromised than before. Life can weaken us, leaving us in pain, exhausted, and self-pitying, when we are carrying beyond our capacity. Our hurt becomes anger, and when bottled up inside, that anger may lead to destructive behaviors. Our unaddressed resentment is expressed as hostility, violence, and isolation. The longer we carry the weight of unexamined losses, the heavier they become. Through the experience of processing,

> The human condition is this: in a broken world, we are all shattered vessels, working to restore shards and sparks to their source.

of coming to understand the sources and manifestations of our pain, we lighten our load and become stronger. We find our capacity for healing, for forgiving, and ultimately for understanding the blessings that come from despair.

Each of us may one day find that the weight of our burdens has become too heavy for us to bear. Many people can recognize the signs of a struggling person only after they themselves have lived through similar experiences. When we encounter another tottering on the verge of collapse, we may acknowledge that we too are vulnerable. We recognize that the inborn strength of that individual's spirit, coupled with the weight of the burdens that individual bears, have left this soul crushed. With humility and compassion we can listen to a story of pain, offering kindness and caring. The human condition is this: in a broken world, we are all shattered vessels, working to restore shards and sparks to their source.

The Tale of the Strudel: *Tzures* and Gratitude

When weighed down by burdens that impose unbearable heaviness on our spirits, we may find that we can no longer carry our sorrows; we are unable to lift up our heads and see the good of the world. We have all experienced the blues or common depression as days when we sense anguish and hopelessness, when we feel that the world does not look right. Common depression is marked by loss of appetite, lack of sex drive, difficulty sleeping and even breathing, a lack of motivation and avoidance of social interactions, difficulty in focusing, and preoccupation with the meaning of life. Common depression can be triggered by holidays or milestones, by monthly hormonal cycles, or by the dark, cold months of winter. It can be brought on by sleep deprivation or an illness that makes an ordinary day seem overwhelming. Young people are particularly susceptible, perhaps due to

inconsistent eating and sleeping patterns, changing relationships, and the search for a path, a purpose. In research cited
by Professor Tal Ben Shahar in his work on happiness, 45 percent of college students experienced common depression in
the course of a year that rendered them unable to function.[30]
Common depression occurs during day-to-day living in the
space between contentment and angst, between expectations
met and disappointments encountered.

Before turning to the question of how despair can reach
a point where we find that we just cannot get up off the
ground, I offer you the following folktale about the worries
and sorrows that we carry. In Yiddish these trials and tribulations are called a *peckel*, a bundle of troubles. This story
reminds us that the burdens that make us feel blue and make
the world appear hopeless are as inevitable as the sunrise or
the change of the seasons.

> A woman says to her rabbi, "My husband lost his job,
> my son is not motivated to study, and I can hardly sleep
> due to worrying about our future. Why is it that so
> many people around me seem contented?"
>
> "Make an apple strudel," the rabbi responds, "and
> take it to your neighbors. Offer the strudel to any neigh-
> bor that you find that has no *tzures*, no problems."
>
> A week later the woman returns with a strudel in
> hand. "Rabbi, I went from door to door and offered the
> strudel on the condition that you told me. *Gutenu*, oh
> my God, such stories! No one qualified for my strudel.
> I never knew that my neighbors had so many problems.
> I told people of my woes as well and felt much better.
> Now, I have made a fresh strudel for you."[31]

From this beautiful little tale we learn that when we are burdened with despair, with the weight of the everyday trials
and tribulations of life, we can share our stories and find

that a portion of our burden has been lightened. When we are struggling with fear, we can listen to a message of empathy and hope. When we are suffering, we can choose to see the world with gratitude and find relief in giving.

Despair Turned Inward: Major Depression

When common depression, the blues, spirals down into major depression, the illness can develop its own course and its own rhythm. Messages of hope do not reach us, deeds of goodness are beyond us. The beauty and kindness present in the world are unseen. The pain takes on a greater spiritual dimension: Why did God do this to me? Why is the world unjust? What am I here on this planet for? Clinical depression often lasts longer than the blues, for two or more weeks. As many as one in four Americans will experience a major depressive episode requiring medical care.[32] Despair in this extreme form feels like drawing in salty water in stormy seas, when the effort just to stay afloat and to take in breaths becomes utterly exhausting.

When we find ourselves in the place of major depression, we grapple with two worldviews. We are rational individuals who know that each day and each life contain beauty and pain, order and unpredictability, light and darkness. And yet, clinical depression involves an element of self-loathing, the sense that the world is broken and we somehow deserve these unbearable burdens imposed upon our fragile backs. This aspect of major depression, the sense of self-hatred and utter worthlessness, is difficult for those who have not experienced it to comprehend. Yet those of us who have been in that place may read this nodding our heads, recalling the feelings of disgust. When we suffer from major depression we are incapable of seeing our own selves as created in the image of God, worthy of love and empathy.

Within this spiral through self-hatred toward collapse, we continue to exist on four levels but our emotions may overwhelm our capacity for rational thought. And when the pain is overwhelming, the sense of injustice unbearable, and the self-loathing intolerable, we may find ourselves driven to behaviors to escape from the pain: overworking, outbursts of anger, abuse of drugs or alcohol, harmful relationships. In the midst of hopelessness and worthlessness, in the depths of a suffocating self-obsession, we cannot hear a message of hope, we cannot recover faith in a world of good or find a purpose. Instead we sink deeper, as the self-hatred and darkness become almost comfortable in their familiarity.

At this point in the momentum of the descent, we can lose the will to change. In time, we may lose the ability to change. We become stuck in the deep darkness. Although we may receive counsel from family, friends, or clergy, we do not take steps toward healing. Our loved ones become frustrated and afraid that this spiral downward has taken on a course that cannot be altered. As the spiral wends its way down and the voice of self-loathing grows obsessive, we lose our perspective on our pain, we cannot understand our loss. We must seek medical help for assessment, diagnosis, and treatment. Despair is an illness—physical, emotional, intellectual, and spiritual. Medicine can make it possible for us to begin to move forward from that stuck place by addressing the level of anxiety or depression that leaves us paralyzed or even in danger. Counseling can allow us to examine the harmful thoughts we have come to accept as truth, to understand our perceptions of ourselves and of our world, and to see that the world is broken but good. We may require rest and calm for our crushed souls to heal.

A word here on the importance of sharing secrets and stories. When we are in a dark place, we tend to isolate ourselves, to avoid interactions, and to hide our thoughts. We may inadvertently alienate family and community. We may be too exhausted, too full of shame, or too certain that no one will understand our suffering. But I have seen in my own life and in my counseling that sharing pain—discreetly and appropriately—can lighten our burdens and bring us hope. Keeping a secret, masking our turmoil, requires a great deal of energy and ultimately contributes yet another burden to our crushed spirits. In my own case, I told my brother and his wife about my pain. Their willingness to listen was a reminder to me that kindness exists in this broken world. Even in my tormented state, I was aware of being loved and found comfort in that love.

Years after I regained my equilibrium, I still felt vulnerable to relapse and did not talk about my experience with deep despair. Yet when I did begin to tell of my spiral into darkness, I was greeted with compassion and a flood of stories. I found hope in stories of those who had suffered and found healing and purpose. The Alcoholics Anonymous program, since its inception in the 1930s, has recognized the power of retelling our stories until we address our

> When we listen actively, we offer humility and compassion, the blessings of despair.

shame, forgive ourselves for our past, and take actions that represent new chapters in our life story. I discovered that behind the doors of loving homes lay pain, desperation, and chaos. When we become listeners, we become aware of the suffering that has been quietly hiding all around us. To listen well is to be open to the suffering of the speaker, without offering judgments or solutions. When we listen actively, we offer humility and compassion, the blessings of despair.

The Anguish That Cannot Be Borne: Suicidal Desperation

For some of us, at some point, depression turns to desperation. When we can no longer bear the burdens we carry, when the pain becomes intolerable, we are in grave danger. Often a state of desperation means that we can no longer function physically in the world, and emotionally we have become numb in response to overwhelming pain. We can no longer make rational, intellectual choices. And spiritually we find ourselves without faith in the goodness of the world, in hope for the future, in a purposeful life. What makes this sickness so complex is that the symptoms may be entirely invisible to the outsider. From that dark place, we may use drugs until we overdose, refuse food until we starve our bodies, and lose our will to live until we succumb to illness. Suicide to the person in a state of desperation represents a means of escaping intolerable pain.[33] I remember in my darkest moments being aware that I loved my family, yet I remained detached from the suffering I was inflicting upon them. The desperate yearning for release from agony becomes the sole focus of the sufferer's thoughts and acts. I could no longer see the world through God's eyes and say: "It is good." There was no place for me in the world. I was certain in my belief that the best course was to end my suffering by ending my life. And I was saved because some small, still voice inside of me chose life.

Shakespeare, with his extraordinary insight into the human soul, understood suicidal yearning. Hamlet expressed his craving for release from his suffering, his yearning for an end to existence acceptable to God, and his view of a world gone rotten:

> O, that this too too solid flesh would melt,
> Thaw, and resolve itself into dew!
> Or that the Everlasting had not fixt

> *His canon 'gainst self-slaughter! O God! God!*
> *How weary, stale, flat, and unprofitable*
> *Seem to me all the uses of this world! (*Hamlet, Act I,
>   Scene II)

In his "To be, or not to be" dilemma, Hamlet longs for an end to the pain of knowing his uncle has murdered his father and married his mother:

> *To die: to sleep;*
> *No more; and by a sleep to say we end*
> *The heartache, and the thousand natural shocks*
> *That flesh is heir to ... (Act III, Scene I)*

The spiraling down and self-loathing of major depression go beyond the familiar blues of common depression. William Styron, author of *Sophie's Choice*, wrote of his ordeal with severe depression in *Darkness Visible: A Memoir of Madness*. He explains:

> Depression is a disorder of mood so mysteriously painful and elusive in the way it becomes known to the self—to the mediating intellect—as to verge close to being beyond description. It thus remains nearly incomprehensible to those who have not experienced it in its extreme mode, although the gloom, "the blues" which people go through occasionally and associate with the general hassle of everyday existence are of such prevalence that they do give many individuals a hint of the illness in its catastrophic form.... The pain of severe depression is quite unimaginable to those who have not suffered it, and it kills in many instances because its anguish can no longer be borne.[34]

Here Styron provides insight drawn from experience on the intolerable pain of deep depression.

As I noted earlier, this book, *Healing from Despair: Choosing Wholeness in a Broken World*, was prompted in part by the loss of my dear friend to an apparent suicide. My friend was known for his caring heart, the time he devoted to others, and his sense of humor. Even those who were closest to him did not detect his desperation. After his death, I could not help but reflect on the last time I had seen him. When we spoke at a rabbis' conference months earlier, I did not notice any signs of his emotional turmoil. After his death I found myself wondering whether I had missed an opportunity to listen more closely, to be a caring friend who could have made a difference.

More people in the United States die each year from suicide than from homicide.[35] Sensitive individuals are particularly vulnerable to despair, as are creative personalities.[36] The damage to the loved ones of each lost soul is enormous because of the unanswered questions, the guilt about how we could have reached out to the soul in pain. After my friend's death, I sought out books to offer me some understanding of the pain that prompts a person to take his or her own life. My own need to understand the spiral down from despair through depression to desperation prompted me to read, to study, and to compose this book.

I began to tell my own story of desperation only gradually. I was encouraged by the words of Art Buchwald, the Pulitzer Prize–winning satirist, delivered at a conference that I attended. He spoke personally and with wry humor of the need to respond to the anguish that leads to suicide:

> They told me that I could speak about whatever I wanted, so I have chosen to speak about depression and suicide. I have been hospitalized twice for depression. The only reason I did not take my own life is that I feared that the *New York Times* would not write my obituary. I am the friend who drove William Styron to the hospital. He wrote about his experiences in the

best-selling *Darkness Visible* but failed to give me a per-
centage of the royalties. He should have. For without
my intervention, he would not have survived to write
the book. Intervention is in some cases necessary. You
need to take seriously the depression of friends. Let
them know that if they take their lives, they will regret
it two weeks later.

Buchwald passed away recently. When he did, his obituary
appeared on the front page of the *New York Times*. By sharing
his story, he contributed to the public discussion of the dan-
gers of depression. He gave me a precious gift: the courage
to tell my own story of illness. He made it clear that when
we talk openly about blues and depression and suicide, we
gain understanding that one day may save a life.

To save a life, the tradition emphasizes, is to save an
entire world. In the context of admonishing a witness to a
capital offense, the Mishnah states: "Only a single Adam
was created to teach you that if anyone destroys a single soul
from the children of Adam, Scripture charges as though the
person has destroyed a whole world" (*Sanhedrin* 4:5). Our
challenge is to see our own lives as precious and to convey
this message to those in pain. When we tell our stories and
when we listen to others, we transform the experience of
deepest despair into an act of great compassion. In the next
chapter I will share my memories of the depth of my own
suicidal obsession. I do so with the hope that my coming forward will provide greater understanding of what Rebbe
Nachman called "bitter darkness" and offer guidance that
may prevent the loss of a world.

Tools for Transformation

Reading Psalms

When we read from the psalms out loud, we find voice for our emotions and we discover the strength that comes of repeating ancient words across time. Psalms are poems to God, at once comforting and hopeful.[37]

Psalm 88:2–19

O Lord, God of my deliverance; by day I cried, at night I stood before You. Let my prayer reach You, incline Your ear to my song. For my soul is filled with troubles and my life is at the brink of the grave. I am numbered with those who go down to the pit, I have become like a man without strength. I am [considered] among the dead who are free as the slain that lie in the grave, those You are no longer mindful of, and who are cut off by Your care. You have put me into the lowest pit, into the darkest places, into shadows. Your anger lies heavy upon me and with all Your waves [of wrath] You have afflicted me. You have estranged my friends from me; You have made me abhorrent to them; I am imprisoned and cannot emerge. My eyes grieved because of such affliction; I have called upon You, O Lord, every day, I have stretched out my hands to You. Will You work wonders for the dead? Will the lifeless rise and thank You? Will Your kindness be declared in the grave? Your faithfulness in destruction? Will Your wonders be known in the dark and Your kindly deeds in the land of oblivion? But as for me, to You, O Lord, I cry, and in the morning my prayer will be early to greet You. Why, O Lord, do You reject me? [Why] do You hide Your face from me? I am afflicted and at the point of approaching death; from youth I have borne Your sudden terrors which have become part of me. I am overwhelmed by Your fierce wrath; Your ferocious attacks have cut me off. They swirl about me like water all the day; they engulf me at once.

You have distanced friend and neighbor from me; from my companions, I am [abandoned] in darkness.

Psalm 139:1–14

O Lord, You have examined me and [You] know [me]. You know my sitting down and my rising, You know my thoughts from afar. My going about and my lying down You have observed, and all my ways You recognize. There is no word on my tongue, alas, O Lord, You know it all. The back and front [of me] You have fashioned and You laid upon me Your hand. Such knowledge is concealed from me, it is too high, I cannot [grasp] it. Where could I escape from Your spirit, or where could I flee from Your presence? If I would ascend to heaven, You are there; and if I were to descend to my grave, You are there. If I were to take wing with the dawn, and dwell in the uttermost part of the sea, even there Your hand would lead me, and Your right hand would hold me. And if I were to say, "Surely darkness will envelop me, night would be as light about me," even the darkness conceals nothing from You, but the night shines as the day; the darkness is as the light. For You have fashioned my mind, You covered me in my mother's womb. I will thank You, for I am awesomely, wondrously made; wonderful are Your works and my soul knows it well.

Writing Psalms[38]

Allow yourself to write from your heart to God expressing your yearnings, fears, and hopes. In doing so, you may find clarity, catharsis, and connection to God and community, as those in the past who have found comfort and care in addressing a greater presence.

Two

Bitter Darkness

In the aftermath of my hospitalization for encephalitis I returned to work. Yet I was unable to concentrate and I was even disrespectful to my boss. I felt inexplicably angry, filled with an indescribable malaise. I now know that I needed time to heal and to understand my direction in life.

What Are We? Where Are We Going?: Wanderings

Tahiti spoke to me of the simplicity and harmony that I was seeking but could not find in my own life. I recalled that the French artist Paul Gauguin spent years in the French Polynesian islands, painting the primitive beauty of Tahitian paradise. Although I was not aware of Gauguin's life story at that time, it is strange to note that when Gauguin began his 1888 Tahitian masterpiece *Where Do We Come From? What Are We? Where Are We Going?* his plan was to take his own life upon the completion of the work.[1] I believed that in Tahiti I would explore my identity, find what work I was called to do, and understand who I was meant to become.

And so, an uncertain and ailing lawyer, I arrived at the dock in Papeete and found work with a French chef from San Francisco who had built his sailboat by hand. The boat's automatic steering mechanism was broken and I was hired to steer the ship through the night from island to island for about ten days. My sweetest memory of that time was of sailing through the night, listening to the music of Keith Jarrett playing solo piano underneath the beautiful sky of stars. It was as close as I would come to experiencing utter calm and quiet joy in the course of what would become more than ten months of wandering. Wherever I traveled, my anxiety, my lack of purpose, and my sense of hopelessness were my constant companions.

During my six weeks in French Polynesia, I began to think of myself as a traveler, an explorer of the world. I did not find tranquility in Tahiti but I did discover the pleasure of adventure, of freedom from commitments, of meeting other world travelers. It was 1981 and the new frontier was Mainland China, where limited group tours with official state guides had become available since President Nixon's visit in 1979. Rumor had it that China was beginning to issue visas on a limited basis to young people traveling independently and that a youth hostel in Hong Kong was arranging these first visas. So I set off for Hong Kong and then China.

By the time I had finished traveling in China close to three months later, I had begun to unravel. In the winter of 1981, China had no signs in English. The locals rarely understood a Western language. Wherever I went, people stared. I remember watching pandas in a zoo and having a crowd form behind me. Apparently most of the visitors to the zoo had never seen an American or European before. During my travels, I delivered a lecture on medicine and law at a Chinese medical school where I was treated as an honored guest. Yet the demands of eleven weeks in China, including a bout with walking pneumonia, wore me down and pushed me to the end of my exotic adventure.

Physically and emotionally exhausted, I decided to rest in Hong Kong before continuing to explore the world. In Hong Kong I was presented with an opportunity that would become an obsession: a contract to coauthor a book, *China Off the Beaten Track*, on the subject of traveling alone and on the cheap in China. Yet, when I began to write, I found that I lacked the ability to focus, to process ideas, and to complete a project. The publisher of the work provided a small apartment in a fishing village on the island of Lantao. While I sat with pen and paper trying to write, I imagined how having my name on a book would create a place in the world for me. And yet, unable to concentrate, I decided instead to continue traveling.

Once I left Hong Kong for Singapore, the book contract became an obsession. The inner debate would lead me around in circles, filling my mind with racing thoughts that I could not quiet. By day I would go through the motions of a traveler—attending a Hindu wedding, visiting a synagogue from British colonial times—but at night I could not fall asleep. I remember lying awake on my top bunk in a dive in Singapore, torn between whether to return to Hong Kong and the book project or to continue traveling, filled with disgust at my indecision.

Shattered in a Broken World: Let Me Just Die

After my first night in Singapore, I told a fellow traveler, an American stockbroker, about my incessant debate. "Let it go," he advised. "Every day I make decisions. Some are wrong but I move on." Although intellectually I recognized that his words made sense, emotionally I could not let it go. The back and forth of my own voice only grew louder when

I sought the quiet of sleep. The end of my travels arrived when all of my cash was stolen from my room in a cheap hotel. Out of money, out of energy, and out of will, after ten months on the road, I was done. A year later, the book would be completed without me and the author would thank me in the acknowledgments.

I do not remember my arrival in my hometown of Phoenix. I only recall being in my own room, the room I had shared with my brother when we were growing up. I was disgusted with myself over my indecision, at what I saw as my defeat at coming home, and at my lack of insight into what I was meant to do with my life. Here I was, exhausted and back at home, spending most of each day in bed, wanting to be alone, shamed by my failure, imprisoned by my thoughts, obsessed by my sense of worthlessness.

My brother, Mark, eighteen months my senior and a physician, represented hope and safety. Perhaps he could pull me up and out of my stuck, painful place. With Mark's encouragement, my parents put me on a plane to visit with him in Houston. I arrived with only enough strength for the most minimal tasks. And strangely, even in that state I could appear polite and reasonably charming while inside I was struggling with my own lack of purpose and sense of failure. One morning, when my brother was at work at the hospital, I revealed to my sister-in-law, Carol, that I was having suicidal thoughts, thoughts that came to me as a yearning that frightened me with their intensity.

When I expressed my thoughts of suicide to Carol, a good listener and a social worker, she and Mark made an appointment for me with a therapist. The next day I found myself in the therapist's waiting room and I began to think: "If I'm diagnosed with schizophrenia or some other psychiatric disorder, it will reflect poorly on my brother, and what will his new wife think of our family? I will just be adding burdens to his life." So I told Carol and Mark, "I am going to the restroom. I'll be right back." And I walked out of the waiting room, out to the street, and away from the office building. I was not looking to hurt myself, but I was certain that I needed to avoid the therapist. I couldn't really reason. I just felt powerless, numbed to thoughts and to emotions. I walked for hours until, exhausted and hungry, I called my brother. I still remember his words to me when he drove up: "Those were the most painful three hours of my life. Don't ever do that to me again." He said it with sorrow and with love. And I responded that I was feeling a bit out of control, experiencing suicidal thoughts, and that I did not want him to be responsible for me. I asked to check into a hospital.

In the morning, we all arrived at the mental hospital and I signed the papers that committed me to the hospital. The administrator and I took the elevator to the ward upstairs and the first thing I saw was a woman screaming as she was dragged down the corridor by two large men. I thought to myself: "This place is for crazy people." My assigned nurse handed me a little cup, ordering me, "Drink this!" I asked, "What is it?" She replied, "Haldol." I knew that Haldol is a chemical tranquilizer, and I thought of it as a medicine that made patients into zombies. The nurse returned with one of the orderlies, who was as big as a football linebacker. "Drink the medicine or we will put you into an isolation room," the nurse stated matter-of-factly. I drank it. But as I did, I had already said to myself, "I'll never take any medicine here again."

I was aware of my growing need to maintain control. The good-old-boy hospital psychiatrist from Texas insisted on devoting our first session to a seemingly irrelevant subject: women I had dated. Remember, this was my first experience with therapy—if you don't count the brief episode in the therapist's waiting room. Even so, it struck me as odd that we were not discussing my indecision and paralysis, my shame and isolation, my pain and hopelessness. Weeks passed at the psychiatric hospital. I was mouthing my pills, hiding them among my socks, where I'd also stashed a credit card, keeping my options open. At this point, I was so physically changed that when we patients were taken to the roof of the hospital to play volleyball, I found that I could not effectively direct the ball. This experience made it clear to me that I was not the person I had been, the athlete who had completed the Boston marathon only several years earlier. I began to plan my escape. As I did so, I was not aware of the parallels with my mother's escape. Only years later did I consider that in my particularly distorted way, I had played out part of her fight for survival, demonstrating my own courage and guile.

The Taste of Ashes: Approaching the Abyss

It was morning at the mental hospital. I put all of my saved pills and my credit card from the sock drawer into my pockets before we descended from our lockup floor. As I returned from breakfast along with the other patients and our chaperones, I stood aside at the elevator and continued walking down the hallway, out of the building. I was amazed to find that I was free, that I was able to walk away by strolling down the street. I felt a certain kind of power, a warped power that allowed me to consider: "Do I finally take my life?" I entered a hotel lobby and at the reception desk requested a room with a view. In this moment, my overriding need was to end the pain, the pain that came from self-hatred and disgust. I did not consider my grieving family or my lost future, but focused only on the moment. I was willing to take any measures to still the throbbing pain, the misery of a world without hope.

I put all of the pills on the nightstand. I walked out on the balcony to see how high up I was. I didn't have a plan. I was confused and in agony. I was disgusted with myself. I was still debating whether and how to act. I struggled. I did not sleep. Exhausted, I tried to doze. Instead, I was pacing to expend the rise and fall of manic energy. I was aware of the taste of ashes in my mouth. I was afraid for myself and at the same time considering taking my life in order to turn off the pain. I was somewhat aware of two distinct voices in my head, one of fear and one of yearning. Sometimes I even spoke my thoughts aloud, like Tevye in *Fiddler on the Roof*. And so passed

> I was willing to take any measures to still the throbbing pain, the misery of a world without hope.

a full day. This was the only time in my life when the act of taking my own life seemed a possibility.

In the morning I called my parents. I needed a break from this debate. My brother arrived just fifteen minutes later. I was relieved to see him and embarrassed. And yet, I also felt defeated by my indecision. Emotionally, I was mostly numb. In this state of isolation, I was not capable of relating to the hurt I was inflicting. I was wracked with pain and all of my energies, thoughts, and emotions were focused on discovering the way to end the misery.

From the Narrow Place: Hope at the New Year

As a rabbi counseling souls in pain during the past twenty years, I have seen how compulsive behaviors can overtake us. When we are in pain, we become controlled by our obsessions. As Dr. Abraham Twerski writes in his book *Addictive Thinking*, "a compulsive act can be irrational, yet the urge to do it may be virtually irresistible."[2] In my work with young people in crisis engaged in harmful, secretive behaviors—drugs or alcohol, violence or running away, unhealthy relationships—I am aware that we will hurt others and lie for our compulsions. In working with tormented adults I have seen how obsession—with alcohol, with an illusion of love, with work—can transform a rational person into a stranger possessed by a craving. The need to maintain a distorted sense of control produces manipulative, dishonest behaviors that alienate loved ones.

> The person we love who is kind and giving still exists, but a soul in the grip of compulsion can be neither honest nor open.

In my case, I had hidden thoughts of my decision to escape from the hospital. It was not a rational course, but a compulsive response to my suffering that came from my own place of self-absorption, from a desperate attempt to assert control. Souls in pain, who find relief in their compulsive behaviors, are not reasonable and are untrustworthy. The person we love who is kind and giving still exists, but a soul in the grip of compulsion can be neither honest nor open. The obsessive need to act in this self-focused way dominates all other impulses.

At my next stop, a Houston teaching hospital, I made no progress under the care of an attractive but inexperienced psychiatric resident. Meanwhile my mother, with her usual resourcefulness and common sense, had found a psychiatrist in Phoenix. Dr. Marty Reiss had at one time considered becoming a rabbi, and was known for his care and skill as a physician. Back in Phoenix, I became a patient in yet another psychiatric hospital. I sought to maintain my own semblance of control: here too I mouthed my pills. Nonetheless, I developed a trusting relationship with Dr. Reiss.

I pause in my narrative to emphasize that those in need of healing may need to go to a hospital to become stable, to rest, and to find the most effective medicines. A good hospital for a suicidal patient offers safety, a therapeutic environment, and a focus on the patient's recovery.

Back to my story. On Rosh Hashanah, the holiday marking the Jewish New Year, the community gathers in synagogue. On a furlough from the hospital, I drove with my parents to the shul where I had spent nearly every Shabbat of my childhood with my father. When it was time to get out of the car, I found I was unable to move. I told my parents what felt very real: "My depression will spread to others by my very presence." Underlying that panic may have been my own shame and fear of being asked what I was doing with my life. When Dr. Reiss heard about this episode, he recommended we consider electroconvulsive therapy (ECT) as the last, best hope for my recovery from deep depression. I was agreeable. I wanted to feel normal again, to have my energy back, to have my life again. And as I was to learn after the ECT, my brain chemistry—under the effects of a depression that had continued unabated for many months—had changed. The impact of ECT would demonstrate to me that our brains are fundamentally chemical laboratories.

My New Worldview:
Countering Depression in the Brain

All of our thoughts are processed chemically. Lack of sleep, genetic predisposition, or crisis can throw our brains into havoc. Some therapists make the distinction between a situational, external cause, and an internal, biochemical imbalance. No doubt, depression in some cases is physiologically determined. But in most cases the psychological and physiological are intertwined. Disturbed thoughts prompt chemical changes. Lack of sleep, for instance, creates a fog obscuring clarity in thought and perception. And a chemical disorder of the brain leads to anxious thoughts that lead to lack of sleep, which leads to greater chemical imbalance.

The rapidity with which ECT lifted me out of my emotional stupor and negative thinking taught me that a chemical imbalance in my brain can determine my emotional, intellectual, and spiritual state.

In a *New York Times* article titled "Shock Therapy Loses Some of Its Shock Value," Jane Brody reports that electroconvulsive treatment (ECT) is currently used to treat more than 100,000 patients per year in the United States.[3] One theory as to how ECT works is that the treatment allows for the release of natural chemicals in the brain, which in turn stimulate the receptors of the receiving cells so they can receive messages more effectively. Patients report a measurable improvement in mood after the first of a typical course of six to eight sessions of ECT, which is usually followed by a course of cognitive behavioral therapy and antidepressant medication under the guidance of a physician. There are potential side effects, such as the loss of memory. For me, fortunately, the loss was only temporary.

> The facts of my life were the same but the self-loathing was gone, and in its place I found an emerging sense of hope and will.

By the evening after my first treatment, I felt consciously lighter, as if somehow the fog surrounding me had dissipated and light was penetrating my own private darkness. I found enough energy to converse with my parents. With each session of ECT the improvement was significant, until at last I returned home. I felt released from suicidal feelings. Over the months recuperating at home, I regained strength and came to see myself as an individual with the ability to effect change. The facts of my life were the same but the self-loathing was gone, and in its place I found an emerging sense of hope and will. I write as a former patient and not as a psychiatrist, and therefore encourage you to consult with a psychiatrist to determine whether ECT is the right course of treatment for you or a loved one. Even though the fog lifted, I was a long way from healed.

Even today, twenty-five years later, the retelling of this chapter in my life makes me feel a little vulnerable, a little sad, a little scared. Yet with hope came new possibilities and a more positive view of the world. Several months after my treatment, my former college roommate, David, invited me to meet him in Los Angeles and I felt ready to venture out from the cocoon of my parents' home. I made one request: "I heard that there is a rabbinical school in Los Angeles. Can we visit it?" There was a part of me that had always been drawn to the rabbinate. In looking back, I am reminded of a teaching of Willhelm Reich's, the noted psychotherapist and colleague of Freud's. Reich said, "If you want to know someone quickly, ask him his earliest memory." That earliest memory for me was arriving home from Shabbat services, singing to the delight of my parents the *Adon Olam* prayer, containing the verse "God is with me, I shall not fear, body and spirit in God's keep." This foundational memory illustrates how deeply my identity was tied to religious expression and Jewish belonging.

When we reached the university, I borrowed David's blazer. The dean of the rabbinical school agreed to meet with me without an appointment. After we had talked for half an hour there was a knock on the door. My friend needed his blazer back for his interview for a surgical residency. I returned the coat, and the dean and I resumed our conversation. The dean invited me to enroll for the next semester on a trial basis, and so I found myself in Los Angeles studying for the rabbinate.

During my months of despair, I never hurt myself despite my yearning to end my inner pain, despite my suicidal ideation. Over the long period of time that I suffered with severe depression, I never formulated a specific plan, nor did I utilize the means available to take my life. I survived. Others are not so fortunate. I have counseled mourners who have lost loved ones to suicide. I know that souls on the brink of the abyss may not give any outward sign of the depth of their pain or the immediate danger. I know, because I have walked in those shoes, that the desire to take your own life is an irrational impulse, not freely or reasonably chosen. The act is a product of an overwhelming desperation to end intolerable pain.

> The desire to take your own life is an irrational impulse, not freely or reasonably chosen.

Tools for Gratitude

The *Modeh Ani* Prayer

The *Modeh Ani*, "Grateful, am I," is recited on awaking each morning:

> Grateful am I before You—dynamic, steadfast Ruler—that You have returned my soul/breath within me graciously, great is Your faithfulness.
>
> In Hebrew: *Modeh ani le'fanekha, Melekh hai v'kayam, she'hehezarta bi nishmati b'hemlah rabah emunatekha.*

You may find that reciting the prayer each morning upon awaking brings you a sense of comfort and a greater awareness of gratitude throughout the day.

The Practice of Quiet Focus

To begin, set aside five minutes each day to sit quietly. Find a chair or stack of pillows that allows you to sit comfortably with your back straight. Use a timer so you know when the time is completed. Chant out loud the word *shalom* (peace) as if it were a three-syllable word (sha-lo-m), using one syllable for each out breath. After several minutes of chanting, sit quietly following the rise and fall of your breath, paying attention to thoughts as they arise and letting them gently pass on their own. Add a minute every other day until you reach twenty minutes a day. The rewards of daily meditation include greater awareness of your thoughts, increased concentration for any task, and a greater sense of calm.[4]

A Daily Prompt

Choose each day one small act for yourself that brings you joy, whether watching a sunset or the indulgence of an ice cream cone. When enjoying, pause to appreciate the goodness offered by life.

Three

Forgiving the Lost Soul

In my counseling, I have seen how an act of suicide leaves mourners with soul-searching, unanswered questions that often begin with the word *why*—Why did she kill herself? Why didn't I see it coming? Why didn't I make a difference? These questions make the mourning period brutal, and they make the process of healing long and difficult. The profound emotional impact presents obstacles to gaining perspective: guilt at not having prevented the death, and anger at the lost one for having inflicted such enormous pain. I have been asked: Isn't taking your own life the most selfish possible act? While I am aware that it is perhaps the most painful deed, I know that it arises in a soul that is detached from the rational. We strive to forgive, to understand the suffering soul who was overwhelmed by the compulsion to end the pain, who lived with a sickness of the soul that rendered rational thinking impossible, and who could not comprehend the harm his or her deed would cause.

I remember the first person I knew who took his life. Sam was just twenty-three, enormously talented as a student and athlete, popular, handsome, the boy who had literally told me at the Jewish Community Center pool, "Anything you can do I can do better." From hindsight, I wondered whether unreasonably high expectations and striving for perfection had led him to feel a sense of failure. When I learned of his death, my first thought in the midst of my profound sadness was, "If I had been his friend, I could have made a difference." When my rabbinical colleague took his life a few years ago, I thought of the last time we had been together, after eighteen years of friendship, and wondered: "Why didn't I recognize his pain? Why didn't I see the clues?"

Two sons recently came to see me with unanswered questions upon the loss of their mother, a woman who had suffered from chronic depression for many years. As they sat before me, the older son asked, "Is it true that Judaism teaches that to take your own life is a major sin? Does God reject my mother for having committed this act?" I responded that a soul who takes her own life does so as a compulsive, irrational act. If their mother could have understood the pain that she would inflict on her loved ones, she would not have taken her life. I answered that the God that I honor embraces their mother and her pain, knowing that it was the need to escape unbearable suffering that drove her to take her life. The mourning rituals performed in her honor would be the same as those for any loved one.

The shock of losing a loved one to suicide is made even more difficult if we believe that even God detests this act. However, a review of the Jewish tradition reveals a God of compassion and understanding. Suicide is tragic, but the person who takes his or her life is not rejected.

To Destroy a Gift from God: Four Portraits from Scripture

Let me use this as an opportunity to tell you more about Judaism and suicide. In the Bible, there are five figures who committed suicide. Strikingly, there is no specific word in Hebrew scripture for suicide, nor is there an explicit condemnation of the act.

The most famous of these personalities is Samson. Betrayed by Delilah, deprived of his strength, and blinded by the Philistines, Samson chose to die rather than entertain the Philistines at a celebration of their god Dagon. In Judges 16:28 Samson called out to God asking for strength to wreak vengeance on the Philistines. With one hand on each of the central pillars of the Philistine temple filled with three thousand people, Samson cried out, "Let my soul die with the Philistines," and pulled down the pillars, killing himself and all the guests present. The Rabbis identified Samson's deed as a heroic death intended to thwart Israel's enemies, an act of *kedushat ha'shem*, sanctification of God's name. A similar categorization is assigned to the demise of King Saul.

Before the reign of King Saul, each of the twelve tribes of Israel, descended from Jacob, which, had its own independent governing system, in most cases led by a judge. During his reign as the first king of Israel, Saul faced two significant threats: constant battles with the Philistines and challenges to his authority as ruler. Saul's life was marked by episodes of irrational fear, by constant bouts of insecurity and self-doubt, and by dramatic mood swings. In his final battle, which took place on Mount Gilboa just south of the ancient city of Beit Shean, he engaged the Philistines in battle (I Samuel 31). The Philistines, his most mighty foe, possessed the metal chariot, the latest development in military technology. In the course of the battle, all three of King Saul's sons were slain, his troops were decimated, and his capture was imminent. He asked his arms bearer to run him through with his sword but the soldier refused. At last, Saul fell upon his own weapon. When the arms bearer saw his king dying, he, too, fell upon his own blade to kill himself.[1]

The Bible tells two other stories of men who took their lives, both of whom saw the futility and shame of their treacherous behavior. Ahitophel was an advisor to King David who conspired with Absalom, the king's son (II Samuel 15–17). Ahitophel and Absalom plotted to overthrow King David in order to secure the throne. When Ahitophel became aware of the impending failure of the coup d'etat, he returned to his native town and hung himself (II Samuel 17:23).[2] Rabbi David Kimche, writing in thirteenth-century France, commented that Ahitophel knew that if he did not kill himself, he would be executed for treason. In another story of palace intrigue, Zimri, a high-ranking officer in the army of King Elah in the ninth century BCE,[3] assassinated the drunken king and ascended to the throne. But his reign lasted only one week. After General Omri was elected king by the Israelites, Zimri recognized that the people rejected his coup. Zimri "entered the hall of the king's palace, and he burned down the king's palace upon himself in fire, and he died" (I Kings 16:18).

These biblical portraits of men who committed suicide present a clear motive in each instance, whether in the context of a loss on the battlefield, vengeance against an enemy, or the threat of capture for committing treason. And more, each man was effectively on the point of death: Samson facing humiliation at the hands of the Philistines, Saul preparing for the attack by the archers, Achitophel and Zimri anticipating execution as traitors to their respective kings.

These cases do not portray the irrational, compulsive need to turn off emotional pain that usually prompts people to kill themselves. What is fascinating is that while we often look to the Bible for guidance on the crises we face, in the case of suicide there is no direct precedent or clear example that reveals to us the Bible's perspective on suicide.

The Evolving Jewish View: The Suffering Soul

In the rabbinic writings, the commentaries on the Hebrew scriptures that began as conversations from the first century BCE, we find that the view of suicide as a sin did not take hold immediately. There are two primary traditional sources of rabbinic writings: the Mishnah, codified in Israel in 225 CE by Rabbi Yehuda HaNasi, Judah the Prince, and the Babylonian Talmud, codified in Baghdad around the year 500 CE. In the six volumes of the Mishnah, which provides a comprehensive guide to Jewish law, we find no discussion of suicide. Even in the later work, the Babylonian Talmud, we find only one explicit condemnation of suicide (*Baba Kama* 91b). In this one instance, offered in the context of a discussion on self-harm, Rabbi Elazar, who taught in Israel at the end of the second century CE, is cited for his interpretation of Genesis 9:5, "But for your own life-blood, I will require a reckoning."[4] In the Babylonian Talmud we also find stories of people who commit suicide that date from Roman times and other periods, all presented without condemnation.[5]

Only hundreds of years later did the rabbinic sages state the legal implications of suicide. The first reference to suicide that appears in traditional legal writing is found in a Talmudic work called tractate *Smakhot*, which scholars date between the third and eighth centuries CE. *Smakhot* sets forth two significant limitations on the mourning rituals observed for a loved one whose death was knowingly self-inflicted. The first limit is that no eulogy may be delivered at the burial. The second is that the traditional ritual in which immediate family members rend their garments as a sign of mourning is prohibited.[6] Yet the guidelines detailed by the rabbinic legal scholars in *Smakhot* specify that other traditional mourning rituals are to be observed in the case of a soul lost to suicide. Burial is required, the community is to form a row of consolation at the burial to comfort the family, and the traditional blessing over the deceased is to be recited. The legal text does not state why a soul lost to suicide is mourned differently, but it implicitly condemns the act.

The Rabbis writing in *Smakhot* use the Hebrew phrase "to destroy oneself with knowledge" (*le'abaid atzmo b'da'at*) to describe suicide. In all cases, the sages assume lack of intent to commit suicide unless explicit proof is available, with the presumption that a person would not take his or her own life knowingly. The legal text states specifically that if a death could have been caused accidentally, two witnesses are required to prove intent to commit suicide. An example of acceptable proof is provided: if a person stated before witnesses, "I will take my life by jumping off the roof," and then that person ascended before witnesses to the roof and fell to his or her death. Even when a death occurs in an unusual manner, such as by hanging from a tree or by falling on a sword, a lack of intent to commit suicide is assumed (*Smakhot* 2:2–5). The wording of this phrase, "to destroy oneself with knowledge," encompasses both the choice of performing the physical act and the mental capacity to form intent. The sages displayed compassion and great insight into the irrational nature of the taking of a person's own life.[7]

> The sages displayed compassion and great insight into the irrational nature of the taking of a person's own life.

The unfolding Jewish perspective on suicide parallels the Christian and Western traditions. The *Anchor Bible Dictionary* notes that the view of suicide as both a sin and a crime developed relatively late in Christian tradition. The Catholic Church by the seventh century had codified excommunication for a soul lost to suicide and had forbidden burial to those who had violated the prohibition of "Thou shalt not murder," as interpreted to include suicide by Augustine already in the third century.[8] As for the Western tradition, a dramatic shift in attitude followed the 1621 publication of Robert Burton's *The Anatomy of Melancholy*,[9] which described the link between madness, melancholy, and suicide, making the case for a sympathetic view of those who had taken their own lives. The impact of this work and the ensuing public discussion are evident in statistics recorded in England: in the mid-1600s, fewer than 10 percent of suicides were judged to be due to insanity; by the 1690s, that figure had risen to 30 percent; and by 1800 all recorded cases of suicide in England were characterized as caused by insanity.[10] Most European countries formally decriminalized suicide in the eighteenth and nineteenth centuries, although laws treating suicide as a crime remained on the books in Western countries including the United States until late in the twentieth century.[11]

Meanwhile, the Rabbis of the Middle Ages took a strong stand against self-inflicted injury and death. Maimonides in his *Mishneh Torah* called for lashes to be inflicted upon a person who injured himself—an ironic punishment indeed.[12] Widely circulated in the Jewish community at the time was the threat intended as a deterrent that a person who took his own life would not be buried in a Jewish cemetery, and in some communities the threat was enforced. Both Maimonides and Joseph Karo in the sixteenth century, two authoritative codifiers of Jewish law, upheld the ruling that forbade mourners from the traditional tearing of garments in a case where the deceased was lost to suicide.[13] Yet Rabbi Jacob ben Asher, a prominent fourteenth-century legal scholar, permitted immediate family to mourn fully for a loved one lost to suicide, including observing the custom of tearing garments.[14]

In modern times, the consensus among rabbinic scholars has shifted away from viewing the lost soul as guilty of blasphemy. Today rabbis emphasize the lack of conscious intention in the act of self-destruction. This approach is reflected in an influential code of Jewish law from 1835, the *Arukh Ha Shulkhan*, in which the author, Rabbi Yehiel Epstein, stated:

> Generally, when someone takes his own life, we blame it on any reason at all, for instance, fear or troubles, or insanity, or the belief that suicide is a better alternative than getting involved in other transgressions. Suicide is truly a remote prospect for a person in his right mind.[15]

In Judaism's approach to suicide, viewed as a whole over more than three thousand years, we find several lessons. First, our bodies are a gift from God and our responsibility is to preserve life. Second, we are vulnerable, subject to despair and unbearable pain that may lead to compulsive, irrational acts. Third, the Rabbis recognized this lack of intent when they referred to suicide as "destroying oneself with knowledge." This awareness led the Rabbis to presume a lack of rational intent and to avoid condemning suicides as intentional, with a wisdom that foreshadowed a much later recognition in Western society that spiritual suffering rendered lost souls incapable of choosing freely.

Spiritual suffering rendered lost souls incapable of choosing freely.

The Aftermath:
Understanding the Unnatural Death

From this brief examination of the biblical and rabbinic traditions, let me return to the sons whose mother had committed suicide. After speaking to them of the evolving Jewish view of suicide, I asked about their mother, seeking to touch on the four different planes of loss. I wanted to learn from them the physical facts, a description of the unfolding of the events. Mourners may find that retelling a story of trauma brings them a sense of closure. I offered comfort as a caring listener, acknowledging the intensity of their anger, guilt, pain, shame, and horror. I wondered about the questions running through their minds: Why didn't I see it coming? Why didn't I do more?

Rabbi Harold Kushner, who has brought comfort to the many readers of *When Bad Things Happen to Good People*,[16] once shared with me that he has in his library an entire shelf of books on the topic of suicide. He said, "You know, all the books seem to say the same thing. The first half of each book provides all the signs to look for to help prevent a suicide from occurring. And the second half of each book says that if a loved one has taken his or her own life, know that you shouldn't blame yourself. And both are true." The way I understand this paradox, from my own experience on the brink of the abyss, is that for a person who is in deep pain and grappling with suicidal thoughts, there is a conflict between the desire to end the pain and the will to live. The soul in pain may effectively mask the internal anguish with everyday conversation or withdrawal. For the observer, the internal struggle is impossible to recognize.

In *A Tale of Love and Darkness*, Israeli author Amos Oz tells of his anger and guilt in response to the loss of his mother to suicide when he was just twelve-years-old. He writes:

In the weeks and months that followed my mother's death I did not think for a moment of her agony. I made myself deaf to the unheard cry for help that remained behind her and that may have always hung in the air of our apartment. There was not a drop of compassion in me. Nor did I miss her. I did not grieve at my mother's death: I was too hurt and angry for any other emotion to remain.... After a few weeks the anger subsided.... As I stopped hating my mother, I began to hate myself. I still had no free corner in my heart for my mother's pain, her loneliness, the suffocation that had closed in around her, the terrible despair of the last nights of her life.... Yet I was no longer angry with her, but rather the opposite, I blamed myself: if only I had been a better, more devoted, son, if I had not scattered my clothes all over the floor ... if only I'd been like everyone else, deserving a mother, too.[17]

Oz knew that the loved ones left behind must grapple with both anger and guilt, because the lost soul gave them no straightforward clues, no clear cry for help, no request for rescue before leaving this world.

I spoke to the sons from my own knowledge of despair and from the stories told to me. I acknowledged that it is only human to grapple with guilt and anger on losing a loved one to suicide. I described how it is only with the perspective of hindsight that we may recognize signs that danger was imminent. I explained that once a family member decides to take his or her life, there is often very little anyone can do to change that decision, especially when the compulsion to end the pain is kept a secret. I observed that with suicide—as with an accident—the family suffers the overwhelming sense that the death could have been prevented, that the tragedy is unnatural. Guilt, shame, and secrecy make healing a complex and difficult process.

Mourning toward Healing: The Stages of Grieving

After a death, mourners usually pass through five stages of grieving: denial, anger, bargaining, depression, and acceptance. Reaching the fifth stage for a death by suicide requires a particularly difficult journey, but acceptance is achievable. Suicide makes us aware of our own vulnerability and fear that somehow the family is predisposed to madness or that all of the family teeters on the verge of unraveling. It brings out a shame that comes with the persistent questions of whether the family somehow could have prevented the tragedy and the belief that it is wrong to take your own life. Suicide stirs up an anger directed toward the loved one who inflicted such pain and toward ourselves for failure to have acted in time.

Jewish tradition for two thousand years has acknowledged that mourning death is a process with its own rhythm. The first phase of mourning, known as *shiva*, meaning seven, takes place during the first seven days following the funeral. During this period the community cares for the mourners, the immediate family members. The Rabbis teach that during the first week, mourners experience a stormy sea of emotions rising and falling and must humbly ride the waves. The second phase of mourning, *shloshim*, meaning thirty, is the period of thirty days following the funeral during which mourners are encouraged by the tradition to refrain from lighthearted celebration, honoring the seriousness of the loss and the heaviness of the time. And with the passage of time, the intensity of the waves of emotion diminishes, although mourners may encounter unexpected moments of emotion, triggered by unanticipated words and places. Although we cannot speed the healing process, we can gain support through the care of community. For all mourners, with the exception of children mourning the death of a parent, *shloshim* ends the formal grieving process.

The final phase of mourning, *avelut*, lasts a full year from the time of the funeral and is observed by children for parents. During this period the bereaved remains in a state of mourning, reciting at each public service the Kaddish, the mourner's prayer, to acknowledge the memory of the loved one and the gift of his or her life.[18] These three periods of mourning remind us that healing from a loss requires the passage of time, openness to messages of love and healing, and engagement in community. Although mourners may experience profound sadness at the loss, and guilt from wishing to have done more for their loved ones, the experience is usually distinct and apart from clinical depression.[19]

Tell Your Friends: More Will Be Revealed in Time

In my role as a counselor, I have learned that each suicide is a unique story, whether resulting from chronic mental illness or emerging suddenly from immediate crisis. Each threat, cry for help, or talk of death must be considered a warning. My own approach in counseling is to err on the side of caution. Remember Art Buchwald's wry advice: "Tell your friends, that if they take their lives, they will regret it two weeks later." Although from the depths of despair the soul in pain may find a message of hope impossible to grasp, nevertheless the words must be spoken: don't give up, more will be revealed, there is hope, the sun will shine again. We are each responsible to speak to a friend and, if needed, to intervene. The danger of self-destruction may pass because often suicide is a sudden, impulsive deed. Art Buchwald had to take action, to drive William Styron to the hospital, because the person tottering on the brink of the abyss is unable to walk away from the danger, lured by the siren song of relief from pain.

It is important to recognize that intervention can save a life. Let me tell you a story of a friend, Bob. One night at home in Los Angeles, Bob got a call from the wife of his friend John in Chicago pleading, "I need you to come immediately. John's been acting crazy, talking about how no one loves him, how the kids and I don't respect him, and muttering how he just wants to die. About an hour ago he stormed out of the house, carrying his pistol." Bob began to pack. While waiting for the cab he called a friend, a recovered alcoholic, and told him the basic story. His friend yelled into the phone, "Call the police!" "But I can't," said Bob. "If he is arrested and it gets into the papers it will ruin his life." "Better a living friend who hates you than a dead friend who loved you," was the reply. Bob called John's wife, who initially resisted, but in the end agreed. Officers found John by his sailboat, a bottle of whiskey on one side, a loaded revolver on the other. They took him to the station and held him until morning without pressing charges. By then, the alcohol and his craving for death had left him. In time, John began to regain his emotional stability.

> We forgive by remembering that our loved one contained holy sparks and by gathering up those sparks so as to identify a legacy of goodness.

From Loss to Forgiveness: Remembering the Holy Sparks

The loss of a loved one to suicide leaves a tangle of emotions. We address betrayal by understanding that the soul we loved was overwhelmed, possessed by compulsion. We come to peace by accepting that our loved one was at once two people: one familiar to us and the other a stranger who was unable to reason due to illness. We forgive by remembering that our loved one contained holy sparks and by gathering up those sparks so as to identify a legacy of goodness. Healing takes time, demanding patience and humility to process loss. By drawing on our collective Jewish memory, we remember that as a people, we come out of the darkness of slavery into the light of freedom. Our individual lives are part of an ancient tradition of emerging from despair with the motivation and capacity to repair the world.

Tools for Forgiving

Journaling

Consider responses to the following questions about your loved one, whether mourning a death by suicide or either a protracted or sudden illness. Set aside a time each day, such as early in the morning or before bed, or each week, such as just before Shabbat or on Sunday night. Putting your thoughts on paper aids forgiveness, healing the broken parts of your relationship, honoring goodness, and integrating another's life into your own as a source of blessing. How would you like this person to be remembered? What do you miss about her the most? What do you imagine he would say if he could speak to you now? What action would she want you to take? How would he want you to live in recalling his memory? What was your loved one's legacy to you?

Letter Exchange

When loved ones die we cannot converse with them, but we can still express ourselves to them. Write a letter to your departed loved one to gain greater perspective and assist healing. Describe the mix of emotions—loneliness, anger, grief, guilt, love—that you are experiencing. As an act of empathy, write back to yourself "as if" you were your loved one responding. Write a final letter back to your loved one. This exercise may be repeated periodically in the course of the mourning process, bringing a profound sense of your loved one's legacy and of your own progression toward healing.

Four

A Healed World

Even after the Israelites had physically left Egypt behind, they struggled with despair. In the desert, during forty years of wandering, they longed for Egypt, for the familiar. Although the exodus from slavery to freedom took days, the healing process required forty years. During those years in the desert, the Israelites tested Moses's patience again and again with their resistance to change, their unwillingness to live with hope and faith in God's plan, and their incapacity to find themselves worthy to enter the Promised Land.[1] It would take a new generation of Israelites to heed the message of God delivered by Moses, to adopt a new worldview of faith, and to claim an identity as a free people. And in time, our collective memory of slavery became the source of our compassion and of our calling to heal the world.

The Ancient Jewish Tradition: From Crisis Comes Birth

Although most of us do heal from despair, our progress is often awfully slow. In our society, where speed and efficiency are valued, we must remember that recuperating from despair is a gradual process. Just as we spiral downward bit by bit, under the weight of cumulative burdens, so too our upward movement may at times seem barely perceptible. When we look all the way back to the darkest time, we may shudder, at once horrified by the pain we experienced and awed that we have emerged from the dark place. We may begin to recognize how, with the gradual experience of healing, came the possibility of willing direction and a sense of purpose.

New beginnings may emerge from crisis. This insight is contained in the Hebrew word *mashber*, used to mean both "crisis" and "birthing stool." A birthing stool in ancient times consisted of a pair of stone supports on which a woman sat upright to allow gravity to aid in the delivery of a baby. The midwife would stand at the ready before the stones to deliver the newborn.[2] The three-letter root of the word *mashber* is shared by the word for "broken." From brokenness and crisis we may find the beginning of greater wholeness. We find the promise in Psalms: "God is close to the broken-hearted, and those crushed in spirit God delivers" (34:19).[3]

> Just as we spiral downward bit by bit, under the weight of cumulative burdens, so too our upward movement may at times seem barely perceptible.

In the history of the Jews, our greatest crises have served as the bases for new and unexpected beginnings. Our foundational crisis, the experience of slavery in Egypt, gave birth to a people willing to enter into a covenant with God at Mount Sinai. Our crisis of identity came with the destruction of the Second Temple, the center of Jewish life for one thousand years, and prompted a new form of worship in the ancient world that was marked by communal prayer. The historic disaster of the expulsion of the Jews from Spain in 1492 gave rise to Rabbi Isaac Luria and his generation of Jewish mystics. And from the horror of the loss of 6 million Jews, from the ashes of the Holocaust, arose the State of Israel. Although we would not wish for crisis or justify the evil perpetrated against us by the good that may have emerged, we can recognize that birth may follow crisis.

The connection between crisis and birth, despair and newly found purpose, was recognized by Rabbi Luria. He acknowledged that as shattered vessels in a broken world, we find our purpose: "The human task is to liberate or raise these lost sparks, to restore them to divinity. This process of *tikkun*, repair, is accomplished through living a life of holiness."[4] We may find ourselves in despair, overwhelmed by darkness, chaos, and solitude, but there is a job for

> New beginnings may emerge from crisis.

us to do: to help repair the world, to find our own purpose in this work. We are not expected to accomplish the entire task. In the words of Rabbi Tarfon, a prominent first-century rabbinic sage: "It does not rest upon you to complete the work and yet neither are you free to abstain from this work" (*Pirkei Avot* 2:21). From our struggle comes a greater capacity to see the world as good, to craft our identity as healers, and to do our part in the work of repair.

The English artist and poet William Blake was described as "cracked in the head." In response a priest friend observed, "Yes, but it is the kind of crack that lets in the light."[5] From Blake's "visions" and "madness" were born an originality and creativity that inspired the Romantic Movement and endure through time.[6] From brokenness may come a path to repairing the world in our own distinctive way. Winston Churchill, prime minister of England during World War II, believed that the darkness that plagued him was part of a divine plan to prepare him to face the evil manifest in the enemy. Although despair can become a source of vision and purpose, creativity and leadership, we must achieve contentment and balance in order to fully realize our gifts.

God's Partner in Healing:
The Rambam's Humility

Stories of those who have emerged from despair offer hope that beginnings and births do arise from crisis and brokenness. Let us begin with Maimonides, the Rambam, who found himself consumed with despair, bedridden for over a year after his younger brother David drowned at sea. After the loss of his brother, Maimonides became responsible for his family, his brother's family, and the debts incurred when his brother's ship went down in the Indian Ocean. The Rambam reframed his identity as a physician, writing important medical works while he continued his scholarly writing on Jewish topics and at the same time served as the private physician to one of the most powerful rulers in Egypt. He guided communities near and far by responding to requests for legal opinions and by composing enduring works of law, philosophy, and medicine. The Rambam went from writing about God to being God's partner in healing.

Rabbi Abraham Joshua Heschel, the prolific twentieth-century theologian, wrote his first book about Maimonides.[7] In the chapter titled "Transformation," Rabbi Heschel examines how the Rambam's calling as a healer was accompanied by a changed worldview. Before the loss of his brother, the Rambam wrote about a world created by God for humanity.[8] After his time of despair, Maimonides wrote of a world that surpasses human control and understanding, in which our own fleeting lives are but a part of a much larger tapestry of creation. As he explained his new worldview: "The right way of looking at things consists in seeing the totality of existing

humanity ... in regard to the interdependence of all Being....
God, the source and essence of all Being, is uniquely good,
all-knowing, and the creator of only goodness."[9]

From Crisis to Calling: Moses and Rachel

For an illustration from the Bible of crisis as turning point,
let us return to Moses. Before Moses's arrival in Egypt, he
tended sheep in the land of Midian. When God called him at
the burning bush to lead the people, Moses objected repeatedly. In accepting the role of leader, Moses models our
responsibilities to face the challenges of life, to encounter
pain in order to do the work of repair. Later in his story,
when his responsibilities drove him to call to God, "then kill
me now" (Num. 11:15), Moses had reached a low point in his
life, a moment of despair.

And yet, in the midst of his hopelessness, Moses wel-
comed God's message, a message directing him to share his
burdens with the seventy leaders upon whom God would
bestow divine spirit. Despite the hardships, Moses chose the
identity of a leader, the shepherd of his people. He chose to
see the world with great humility: "and the man Moses was
very humble, more than any on the face of the earth" (Num.
12:3). Moses throughout his life continued to encounter
challenges and struggles. He persisted in bearing the weight
of leadership despite the frustration of guiding an often
untrusting, ungrateful people. In a scene from late in
Moses's life we find him once again in crisis, at the breaking
point. He shouts at the people, calling them rebels, asserts
that he and Aaron could effect a miracle, and defies God's
direction to speak to the rock to bring forth water, instead
striking the rock twice (Num. 20:7–12). On the road to healing we encounter obstacles and setbacks. In the case of
Moses, God denied him entry into the Promised Land. Yet,
Moses's greatness as a leader is demonstrated by the totality

of his life, in which he repeatedly overcame despair and renewed hope. With admiration and affection, the Rabbis call him *Moshe Rabeinu*, Moses our teacher.

Rachel, one of the four matriarchs of the Israelites, found a practical solution to her crisis of infertility. She chose help, she chose a new identity as a mother by surrogate, and she chose to see the world with hope and gratitude. Instead of railing against God because she remained barren while Leah continued to deliver sons, Rachel adjusted her expectations to respond to her crisis. Rachel's patience and resilience would enable her to become a mother of two sons through her handmaid and surrogate, Bilhah, and in time to give birth to two sons, Joseph and Benjamin.

Rachel's persistence in the face of infertility would lead the prophet Jeremiah to portray her as the source of compassion and hope for a later generation. Jeremiah imagines a scene in which Rachel weeps for the exiles of Israel after the destruction of the First Temple[10] and God responds to her with the assurance that her people would return to their country (Jer. 31:15–17). Even in our own day, women make pilgrimage to pray at the tomb of Rachel, located near Bethlehem, in search of her comfort and with hopes of her intervention. Rachel is identified with compassion and fertility, with birth and spiritual renewal. She who experienced bitter darkness became a source of light that continues to illuminate and offer hope.

> On the road to healing we encounter obstacles and setbacks.

Sacred Sparks in Each Soul: Rebbe Nachman's Points of Light

Moving ahead in time to the age of modernity, to the nineteenth century, we find Rebbe Nachman of Breslov, who suffered a profound darkness of spirit.[11] Some of his despair was undoubtedly caused by external factors: Rebbe Nachman lived in Ukraine at a time when the Jewish community suffered from extreme poverty and constant oppression. Nachman offered the following guidance for perceiving light amid darkness:

> When a person finds that he is utterly unable to pray or even to open his mouth on account of the greatness of his sadness and the bitterness of the darkness, he may perceive himself to be at an unfathomable distance from the Holy One. Even in this hopelessness he should search and seek within himself a point of merit. He should revive and rejoice through this because surely every person is worthy to grow in joy very greatly from each and every good point within himself. When we are in despair, we look at ourselves and see only unworthiness, but if we search within ourselves for one small point of light, that is good, that is worthy, we will find the one point and then we must search and find another, and then another.[12]

Nachman introduces a play on words, based on the Hebrew word *nekudot*, which means both "points" and "musical notes," to suggest that in setting forth our good points we discover our unique, inner melody.[13] Nachman's profound understanding of that place of "bitter darkness" from which all appears hopeless gave him the capacity to guide his fellow sufferers to perceive the goodness within each person and within the world.

When Bad Things Happen to Good People: God's Place in Suffering

For many of us, our failure to identify our good points comes from the belief that God is afflicting us. A woman told me of a childhood marked by her father's alcoholism, leading her to a series of abusive relationships with young men, all of which left her feeling worthless. Since her parents had taught her that God directed all the events in each life at every moment, she half-believed that God was testing her with trials to purify her soul. After years of suffering, she was prepared to take her life in order to defy this uncaring God and to end her pain. She studied different methods, gathered the necessary materials, and left all of her savings in an envelope marked with the name of a friend. And yet, at the moment she was to act, she found that she could not go through with self-destruction. Afterward, she began the healing process with medicine, therapy, and a message from a rabbi.

In this woman's story, her moment on the brink of the abyss became a turning point. After deciding that she would live, she found a new way of understanding God in Rabbi Harold Kushner's *When Bad Things Happen to Good People*. She found a message that challenged her worldview: God is a caregiver who does not want his children to suffer and each one of us is a child of God. Rabbi Kushner's book emerged from his own experience watching helplessly as his beloved son, Aaron, moved slowly and inevitably toward his death. When Aaron was diagnosed at the age of three with a fatal genetic disease that causes rapid aging, Rabbi Kushner found a need to pray to God and to seek comfort. Yet he refused to pray to a God who would inflict such suffering upon a child. When he turned to the Book of Job, Rabbi Kushner reinterpreted God's words to Job as an expression of God's own limitations. God never answers Job's challenge: "Where is the justification for suffering in the world?" God responds with a description of the grandeur of creation. The conclusion that Kushner drew was that although God exists as a comforting presence, God does not intervene to change nature or the sources of suffering.

The concept of a God with limits appears in the ancient Jewish tradition. Already in the Talmud, codified more than 1,500 years ago, the Rabbis ask: Why does a stolen seed planted by a thief grow? And why is it that a woman who is raped may become pregnant?[14] The questions arise because the Bible presents God as speaking of actively rewarding and punishing, as in the verse, "If you follow my laws and are careful to keep my commandments, I will provide you with rain at the right time so the land will bear its crops and the trees of the field will provide fruit" (Lev. 26:3; Deut. 11:13). If God uses nature as a reward for human behaviors, then we might expect that a just God would mete out punishment to the thief by preventing the stolen seed from growing. The Talmudic scholars answer their own question: "The world operates according to its order." The implication here is that God created a good world, directed by a system of laws. In a world that operates according to its order, prayer is not meant to change God's decision but to allow us to foster a relationship with God.

In Genesis we find a world that God repeatedly views as "good" but never "perfect." In the course of nature's unfolding, bad things may happen. God may choose self-limitation. It is our role to act to fulfill a vision of a world that is just. In Rabbi Luria's description of creation, God is left incomplete once the divine sparks left behind have become intermingled with the shards of the shattered vessels. And although the world is incomplete, we are to acknowledge the order, to see the goodness, and to be awed by the miraculous. We are to partner with God in the work of repairing the world. The healing of the world begins with the work of healing ourselves.

Message, Identity, Worldview: My Choices

Now, some twenty-five years after my crisis, I live with many responsibilities and with contentment. My healing process involved identifying the burdens taken on over my lifetime and acknowledging my strengths and vulnerabilities. Processing my emotional collapse involved years of dedication: openness to counseling, willingness to undergo doctors' care, commitments to exercise, finding a place in community, and retelling my story. This book, too, is part of my ongoing work of owning my story. Over time, my crisis became my turning point, the moment from which I began to move toward who I am today.

As shattered vessels, we are works in progress, studying our past to reinterpret events and looking forward to identify new purpose. Even while we struggle with despair, choices remain open to us. In the depths of despair I could not exert my will. I felt unable to make choices and felt certain that I could not effect change. Healing begins by making small decisions, acts of will, and taking little steps forward.[15] Choosing to go to Los Angeles to meet a friend felt like a big decision. From that first choice a world of possibilities opened up to me: choosing to identify as a rabbinic student and choosing to see the beauty of this new path. Despite my limited concentration, my sensitivity to slights, and my lingering impatience, my rabbinical school studies allowed me to express a core part of my self. Illness offered me a crisis from which to begin anew, to find what I really wanted to do.

To emerge from my crisis with healing and purpose, I needed to understand the trauma of my illness and identify the accumulated weights that had contributed to my collapse. The school therapist, Dr. Ian Russ, offered me a safe healing space in which to grow. During the first session I described my low-grade anxiety, my difficulty in focusing, and my bout with encephalitis. He asked me about my relationship with my father. "I am not sure what you are asking," I responded. "Do you have a book that I could read to understand your question better?" I now smile when I consider how guarded I was emotionally. After a session of therapy, I often found myself feeling depleted and even more anxious. Yet over time, my awareness of my fears and of my unreasonable expectations increased and I achieved greater calm and appreciation of my strengths. I learned to embrace both the striving to meet goals and the feeling of satisfaction even when falling short of the goal. The work of therapy was giving new interpretations to events of the past. This process is comparable to the rereading of a sacred text, uncovering new meanings of the same familiar words. At times I fell back into the pit of self-loathing, chastising myself for needing another's help. And yet, with the guidance of a caring professional, I healed.

> The work of therapy is comparable to the rereading of a sacred text, uncovering new meanings of the same familiar words.

Another piece of healing for me was physical. Over time, it became clear to me that the return to normal functioning of my brain was facilitated by ECT and was necessary as the starting point for my healing. *I cannot state too strongly the importance of medicine prescribed by a physician in treating depression to allow a person to feel stable enough, strong enough, and calm enough to begin healing.* Everything we experience is filtered through the chemistry of our brain. Consider how you see the world when you have the flu, magnified many times over, and that is the distortion of severe chemical imbalance in the depressed mind. For most of us, healing from depression is a process that includes working with a compassionate therapist. Finding the right counselor may require a good deal of trial and error. The healing process may require medication, and determining the right medicine or combination of medicines may require a good deal of trial and error. Be patient and persistent. We are complex beings. The healing process is unique to each individual.

When to Accept Help: The Role of Medicine

Some people suffering from despair are very reluctant to take any medicine. They fear a loss of their ability to make decisions for themselves, a loss of creativity, a loss of emotional joys and sorrows, a loss of sexual drive, a loss of independence from medicines. Some of these fears are legitimate. There are potential side effects associated with all medicines. But for many people struggling with depression, effects that result from the decision not to take medicine are more dangerous. A specialist in psychiatry is qualified to diagnose depression and other mood disorders, to discuss a course of treatment, and to prescribe medicine. Medicine can help reestablish the natural functioning of the brain, helping to return the brain's chemistry to a normal state.

As is often the case with new drugs, antidepressants were discovered by accident. In the early 1950s, while researching an anti-tuberculosis medicine, doctors noted that the agent, isoniazid, seemed to positively impact on mood. Cincinnati psychiatrist Max Lurie termed this agent an *antidepressant*, a designation that caught on widely beginning in the 1960s. Isoniazid became the forerunner of an entire class of medications termed *SSRIs* (selective serotonin reuptake inhibitors), which are the medicines most widely prescribed for depression today. Among the better-known brand names of SSRIs are Paxil, Prozac, and Zoloft.[16] These drugs work by aiding the efficacy of serotonin, a chemical that occurs naturally in the brain facilitating the transmission of signals between neurons. In contemporary medicine, research continues on how neurotransmitters work and on finding new medications that aid in overcoming depression.[17]

The side effects of medicines need to be considered in the decision-making process. A retired friend of mine, under the guidance of a psychiatrist, began taking antidepressant medicines for anxiety so severe that it limited his ability to work. He regained his stability, clarity, and creativity, but he did suffer a significant side effect: he felt certain that his emotional capacity was significantly compromised. He told me a story to illustrate this point. Once while he was at his psychiatrist's office, another patient arrived at the door, threatening to shoot the doctor. The doctor jumped under his desk, the doctor's receptionist hid behind a bookshelf, but my friend remained remarkably calm and simply stood against a wall. When the police eventually arrived and arrested the man, the doctor and his receptionist emerged from hiding, drenched in sweat. "You see," said my friend, "the medication doesn't allow me to experience life fully." And yet a psychiatrist on hearing this story responded to me, "While it's true that medication may limit emotional range, it allows individuals suffering from depression or anxiety to have a breadth and fullness of life that otherwise would not be available to them. Overwhelmingly, my patients choose medicine for the right reasons."

Here is a story I heard in my counseling of the danger of refusing medicine for someone suffering from ongoing depression. For twenty years, a woman in recovery from alcoholism followed a twelve-step program, attended counseling, and took doctor-prescribed antidepressants. As her children grew older she became determined to live "without chemicals." Without a doctor's guidance, she weaned herself from her medicine. Within weeks, she found herself struggling with despair, and sought the numbing effects of alcohol. For four months she was drinking excessively and her life quickly began to unravel. With the support of her husband, she returned to her physician, her program, and her medicine. This story is not intended to demonstrate that patients on antidepressants can never stop taking medicine. However, for some people who are diagnosed with despair, the antidepressant medication provides the chemicals needed to return the brain's balance, just as insulin allows the diabetic to achieve a healthy balance when the body is unable to produce insulin in sufficient quantity. *All decisions regarding the type and dosage of prescription medicines need to be made in consultation with a physician.*

How I Healed: The Slow Spiral Upward

After I experienced the changes made possible by ECT, I spent many years gradually ascending the spiral of healing. On the physical level, I began to run again. In doing so, I found that I began to reclaim not only my energy, strength, and endurance but also my own sense of "willfulness"—the ability to choose commitments and responsibilities and to prove consistent and reliable. The discipline of running gave me confidence that I could actually set a goal and attain it. I found that sweating literally cleansed me of anxiety. I could not have run when I was severely ill. But as I began to heal, I could run, and in doing so, I healed more. Exercise serves as a natural remedy, allowing us to set achievable goals and release natural brain chemicals that create a sense of well-being. Short walks are a place to begin. The purpose is to set and meet achievable goals.

At the emotional level, I learned to be attentive to my emotional state. Healing requires us to feel our feelings. A study of people who contemplated suicide by jumping from the Golden Gate Bridge found that those who chose not to jump shared one common characteristic: they had cried while standing on or near the railing.[18] For me, experiencing my emotions involved acknowledging that life has cruelty, even evil, which meant openly addressing my parents' experiences as Holocaust survivors. My father's silence regarding his war experiences, his choice to distance himself from searing memories, had prevented me from gauging his pain and modeled a kind of emotional distancing. As for my mother, I cannot recall whether I was thinking about her escape from the slave labor crew when I walked out of the hospital to freedom. And yet I had been aware since my childhood that my mother had shown great courage, hoping beyond hope that she was meant to live. I believe that her choice nearly forty years earlier was present in my mind when I did escape and when I chose life. For me, examining my emotions about my parents' suffering and my own responsibilities to carry on my family's legacy was crucial to the healing process.

Prayer also played a role in my healing. Reciting the Hebrew words of the daily morning prayers offered a sense of belonging, connecting me to an ancient people with a long history of countering despair with hope. Certain phrases from the traditional prayer book, such as "God with goodness renews the work of creation each day continuously," reminded me to live life with fresh awareness and gratitude. On some occasions, I would pray with my own words, opening my heart to express hopes, fears, and gratitude. When I prayed to God, I found, like Job, an enduring, caring, divine presence receiving my words.

Healing requires us to feel our feelings.

After my illness, which in many ways centered around my search for identity, I chose a new name, or actually took ownership of my original name. When I was born my parents named me Lazar in Yiddish and Eliezer in Hebrew to honor my great grandfather. My parents chose my English name, *Larry*, because it was the only name beginning with the letter L that they knew. Larry was a regular breakfast customer at my parents' café in Phoenix. But the name never sat right with me, it never seemed to fit. When I was a college student, I read a letter that Elie Wiesel had written and signed with his Hebrew name, *Eliezer*. I said to myself, "That's my name. I will use the name *Elie* too." I identified with Elie Wiesel's testimony of Holocaust survival and his prophetic calls of conscience. And while I was a student in rabbinic school I legally changed my name to Elie. It felt as if I had at last claimed my own identity.

I healed as a member of a community. In the course of healing, we may isolate ourselves, believing that no one can understand our experience of suffering, our state of brokenness. And yet community is the antidote to isolation and despair. My community of fellow students offered belonging in shared meals, study, and prayers. And more, in studying sacred text with my classmates, I found that I had

> Doing for others allows us to reclaim our dignity and to make a difference—important ingredients in healing.

become part of the ancient community of Torah students, conversing across the continents and through the centuries. The traditional communal rhythms, repeated over the course of each day and throughout the Hebrew calendar cycle, and the observance of *kashrut*, Jewish dietary laws, allowed me to reclaim a fundamental piece of my identity.

In healing, I began to accept the responsibility to be present for others. Jewish practice offers what those in despair often need: opportunities for participation, along with required duties. In Judaism, for instance, each individual can become a blessing to others by accepting the responsibility of participating in a minyan, making it possible for a group of ten Jewish adults to formally read Torah and to pray fully, including the mourner's recitation of the Kaddish prayer. In the Jewish tradition we are called upon to visit the sick, to comfort the mourner, to support the orphan. Doing for others allows us to reclaim our dignity and to make a difference—important ingredients in healing.

As we heal, we begin to reclaim the discarded pieces of our identity. During my crisis, entering my family synagogue on the holy day of Rosh Hashanah seemed dangerous and threatening. Looking back at my fear of entering that shul, that place of worship, I see how despair may manifest itself as a rejection of all we hold dear, of our most sacred values. I come from a family that held education, community, and hope as core values. In a sense, I rejected my identity, only to reclaim it as I healed. With time I accepted, as the Rambam had recognized long ago, that in times of affliction we need loving people for comfort. As I healed I reclaimed core pieces of my own identity, including my place amid a loving family and the legacy of the Jewish tradition.

Healing engenders purpose and purpose engenders ever greater healing. My own sense of progress in emerging from darkness came from my growing conviction that I was at last pursuing my calling. When I use the term *calling* I do not mean that I heard God's voice speaking to me. Instead, I felt that somehow my studies addressed and explored the deepest part of my identity. At last I could pursue what I wanted to do and felt meant to do, rather than what I was supposed to do. At last I could be a healer, a caregiver, even a servant of God—living up to my Hebrew name, *Eliezer*, meaning "my God is help" or "helper of God."

> A calling is the work we do in healing the world by using our individual gifts.

Although in my darkest moments I could not have seen the path to rabbinical school, my experience with despair led me to study Jewish text and engage in Jewish practice. A calling is the work we do in healing the world by using our individual gifts.

Modern Heroes: Manifesting Light from A Place of Darkness

In recent times we have seen dramatic examples of people who encounter tragedy, champion a cause rooted in that experience, and ultimately contribute to healing our world. Actor Christopher Reeve, who among many roles played Superman in four films, is such a role model.[19] An avid sportsman, Reeve was participating in a cross-country horseback riding competition when he fell off his horse landing headfirst with the weight of his 215-pound body. This crushed his two upper vertebrae, severing the connection between his head and spine. In the intensive care unit, aware that he might never walk or move any limb again, he considered suicide. His wife, Dana, assured him, "I will be with you for the long haul, no matter what. You're still you. And I love you." Those words, combined with the image of his children, put suicide out of his mind. Yet he continued to struggle with anguish, especially when he was alone at night.

One day as he lingered in the hospital's ICU, a man with glasses entered his room wearing a yellow surgical gown and a blue scrub hat. He said that he was a proctologist and was going to perform a rectal exam on Reeve. The "physician" was Robin Williams. Reeve said, "For the first time since the accident, I laughed." They had a long conversation and Williams told Reeve that he would do anything for him. Reeve would later say that the support of family and friends gave him the desire to live despite his paralysis.

After surgery and months of intensive, arduous physical therapy, Reeve gained the ability to breathe without a respirator and to move a finger. Over time, he returned to work: acting, directing, producing, and writing two books. Aware that the media was following his plight, he decided to make use of the publicity to benefit others with spinal-cord injuries. He lobbied the U.S. Congress for better health-insurance coverage for those with catastrophic injuries and challenged the attendees of the Academy Awards to make more films addressing social issues. He lent his name and resources to generate funding to conduct research on spinal-cord injuries and to create care facilities to allow survivors to live with greater dignity and independence.

A year before his death, he traveled to Israel at a time when the State Department had issued a safety advisory against such visits. His courage prompted many others to consider such travel; but more, his smile, perseverance, and sense of mission inspired those he met who were living with paralysis to believe in their own dignity. Less than a month before he died of complications from infection, California voters approved Proposition 71, for which Reeve had actively campaigned. It allocated $3 billion for stem cell research, offering the hope of new treatment for spinal injuries. In the face of his own challenges, Christopher Reeve had become Superman.

"Candy" Lightner transformed her grieving into action after her thirteen-year-old daughter, Cari, died from injuries caused by a collision with a drunk driver. Despite four previous convictions for driving while intoxicated (DWI), the hit-and-run driver who killed her daughter received only a two-year sentence, which he was permitted to serve outside of prison. Shocked by the failure of the judicial system to adequately punish the guilty and protect the innocent, she vowed to make a difference. In her own words, "[I] promised myself on the day of Cari's death that I would fight to make this needless homicide count for something positive in the years ahead." Her response to senseless tragedy took shape as MADD, Mothers Against Drunk Driving.

In the years that followed, she addressed Congress, appeared on national television, and spoke to local civic and professional groups on the need for just and effective legislation relating to drunk drivers. She offered support to fellow survivors of drunk driving tragedies. Chapters of MADD were organized in all fifty states and other countries with the goals of providing education and preventing, deterring, and punishing drunk driving. She served as president of MADD for the organization's first eight years. In the twenty-five years since MADD was founded, alcohol-related traffic fatalities in the United States have been reduced by 40 percent, saving more than 300,000 lives.[20]

In Israel in 2001, the thirteen-year-old son of American-born parents who chose to live and raise a family near Jerusalem was murdered when terrorists smashed his head with rocks in a cave not far from their home. The loss of Koby devastated his parents. With the kindness of caring neighbors, faith, and the need to care for their children, they moved forward one day at a time. Koby's mother, Sherri Mandell, poured out the sorrow of her first year of mourning in her book, *Blessing of a Broken Heart*.[21] In time, she and her husband established a foundation dedicated to alleviating the isolation of others in Israel who had lost loved ones to terrorism and created Camp Koby for children impacted by terrorism.

Not everyone can transform losses into public acts of healing, but these stories demonstrate the human capacity to emerge from devastating events and build on tragedy to serve others. Thus, each of us, by simply allowing our dark past to reach the light of day, can become a powerful source of healing. When I spoke last year to a group of rabbis in Los Angeles about despair and the Jewish tradition, sharing for the first time in public my own history of hospitalization, I felt that it represented a coming out. I found that in speaking openly, I experienced a sense of relief, of gratitude for my healing, and of greater acceptance that despair is a natural part of life. Some of those present thanked me for my honesty. Others told me that my public disclosure had given them greater courage to reveal their own stories of despair with greater acceptance of their own times of darkness. Telling and retelling our stories allows us to heal from our shame and to forgive ourselves for our times of despair, for succumbing to hopelessness.

The Gift of Love in Healing

There is one more important element in my unfolding story, and that is love. One year after I had begun rabbinic studies, my brother Mark—who had cared for me with such constancy—called me to announce: "I found your *kallah*, your bride. When she speaks, she reminds me of you." It was not easy to accept my big brother telling me whom I was going to marry. Meanwhile Mark was telling Linda, a neurology resident working with him at Columbia's Neurological Institute, "You have to meet my brother." When Linda was scheduled for a layover at Los Angeles airport, I told her I would meet her at the gate wearing a straw hat. When she arrived she walked right past me, then came back and introduced herself. We talked about our love of travel and our shared dream of visiting Nepal. I even suggested, "Maybe one day we can go to Nepal together." Over the months we talked on the phone, and when I visited her in New York, I told her about the story of my collapse.

Although we had spent only twenty-one days over several months in each other's company, I asked Linda to join me in Jerusalem where I would continue my rabbinic studies. She did, and a few months later, we were engaged. The moment when I proposed to Linda in the garden of

Jerusalem's Ticho House, a stately Turkish home from the time of the Ottoman Empire, was a milestone I never could have imagined in my days of darkness.

As we heal, we accept commitments. Fulfilling these commitments gives us a sense of our capacity to achieve goals that in turn allow us to heal more fully. If I had met Linda before my collapse, I would have appreciated her beauty, kindness, and talents. But after my crisis, I was grateful to her for something much more powerful. She knew my past and chose to accept me. Up until then, even with my progress, I still saw myself as damaged goods, as less than whole. I had not yet forgiven myself for my vulnerability, my self-hatred, my acts of selfishness. When we became engaged, I realized that I could be present for another person and that this lovely, accomplished woman considered me worthy of her love. Now looking back, after over twenty years of marriage, I can see that my willingness to enter into marriage represented my capacity to accept my own flawed self, to take on commitments, and to live a life committed to others.

To Every Thing There Is a Season: Processing Loss

From my experience in counseling, I have become aware that there are different phases to both crisis and healing. In the words of Ecclesiastes (3:1–5):

> Everything has its season and there is a time for every-
> thing under the heaven
> A time to be born and a time to die
> A time to plant and a time to uproot that which is planted
> A time to kill and a time to heal
> A time to tear down and a time to build up
> A time to weep and a time to laugh
> A time to wail and a time to dance
> A time to scatter stones and a time to gather stones together.

When I meet people who are suffering from the pain of loss, I think of Ecclesiastes' teaching that there is a time for healing, and, I would add, healing takes time. The recognition that the passage of time is necessary for healing informs the Jewish practice of observing the mourning periods of *shiva*, *shloshim*, and *aveilut*. The tradition acknowledges that while each individual's grieving follows a distinctive rhythm, the structure of rituals may guide and support us toward healing.

> There is a time for healing and healing takes time.

My approach to counseling seeks to support active processing, a way of coming to understand the nature of our loss at each level. When we do not process a loss, we often avoid the future and yearn for the past. When we do not process a loss, we often expend a great deal of energy suppressing the pain, leaving us with less emotional capacity for spontaneous joy and empathy. When we do not process a loss, we often find our hurt becomes anger, which is released as outbursts of temper or destructive behaviors. When we do not process a loss, we often harm others unwittingly, so filled with our own thoughts that we cannot consider the troubles of others. When we do not process a loss, we remain slaves to our despair and fail to see crisis as a source of new beginnings. And, when we do not process a loss, the hostility can become directed at ourselves, so that we lose the sense of who we are and what we are capable of becoming. To integrate our loss we must consider our perceptions, thoughts, feelings, and yearnings and finally come to see the world as good.

Healing to the Point of Forgiving: Ourselves and Others

A story of forgiveness that has had a great impact on me was told to me by a congregant about her father's death. The daughter, a nurse, had come to me and asked for guidance in offering a caring presence at her father's deathbed, given her father's past cruelty to her mother. I offered her the wisdom of Rebbe Nachman that she seek out a single good point in her father, a characteristic that reflected the spark of the divine within him, even if it had not been fully realized. I suggested that she consider his own despair at his flaws, failings, and shattered state and in the end, I asked her to embrace him with compassion. A week later she called me from her father's deathbed: "I am sitting here holding my father's hand. He just died. And I was able to be fully and compassionately present for him. I found points of goodness in him, qualities that reflected God's image. And when I said to him, 'It's okay, you can go now,' he did, he died within moments."

> To forgive is to acknowledge that we have shortcomings and yet are worthy of love.

Healing fully requires we realize our capacity to forgive others and ourselves. Whether we are caught in the spiral of deep despair that fills us with self-loathing or are overwhelmed by resentment and bitterness directed toward others, to forgive is to let go of much of the anger that we hold on to. Anger is like a torch we cling to only to find that the flame has burnt us. To be able to forgive is to move from anger to acceptance. To forgive is to acknowledge that we have shortcomings and yet are worthy of love. From that place of humility we remember that we all are capable of committing wrongs. And yet that fragility is part of what it means to be human.

Tools for Healing

Rebbe Nachman's Points

Bring to mind a person who has done you wrong. Examine his or her deeds and identify just one act that evidences goodness. Search and find another point of goodness and then another. Connect the dots, revealing an image of goodness. Put into perspective the wrong done within the larger tapestry of the wrongdoer's life. Allow yourself to forgive by embracing the wholeness of the other.

Forgive Yourself

Examine yourself and find an act or attitude of goodness. Do not be too quick to dismiss your deed as prompted by selfish motives. Examine within the deed, finding a point of goodness. Continue reviewing your deeds, finding another and still another point of goodness. Connect the dots and allow yourself to value your foundational goodness. Make a commitment to more consistently act with goodness and with more selfless motives in the future.

Five

You Shall Be
a Blessing

The Torah tells the story of the Israelites framed by three key events: creation of the world, liberation from slavery, and the revelation of the Ten Commandments. The moment of revelation at Mount Sinai represents the critical point in the story, the moment at which the relationship between God and the people becomes a commitment. This relationship of covenant is first mentioned in the story of Noah, but is presented more completely and as an agreement of mutuality in the story of Abraham, who is identified as the first Jew.

Deeds of Charity and Justice:
Abraham's Compassion

God says to Abraham, "Go from your land, from your birthplace, and from your family home, to the land that I will show you. And I will make of you a great nation, and I will bless you and I will make your name great and you shall be a blessing" (Gen. 12:1–2).[1] God's initial call to Abraham marks the beginning of his life as a wanderer and offers Abraham a purpose: to become a blessing. Years later, after Abraham establishes himself in the land that God had shown to him, the land of Canaan, God speaks to Abraham of the covenant. The terms of God's covenant are that Abraham will be faithful to God and God will make Abraham a father of a multitude of nations and will give Abraham's descendents the land of Canaan (Gen. 17:3–8, 18:19).

Abraham fulfills the covenant by leading a life of compassion. In a familiar image of the patriarch, we find Abraham sitting at the entrance of his tent during the hottest part of the day. He notices three strangers approaching and runs to greet them, bowing before them and offering, "My Master, please, if I have found favor in your eyes, please do not pass from before your servant. Let some water be brought to wash your feet. Rest under the tree. I will get a morsel of bread for you to refresh yourselves, then you can continue on your way" (Gen. 18:3–4). Abraham's language is marked by humility and his actions demonstrate his eagerness to be of service. It is precisely Abraham and Sarah's experience as wanderers that moves them to serve strangers. Abraham and Sarah understand that offering kindness to a stranger is a form of serving God. With their commitment to open their home to those in need of shelter and food, Abraham and Sarah become a blessing to strangers in their midst.

The true measure of Abraham's commitment to following God's ways is presented in the story of Sodom and Gomorrah. The Torah records God thinking aloud while preparing to destroy the inhabitants:

> Shall I conceal from Abraham what I do, now that Abraham is surely to become a great and mighty nation, and through him all the nations of the world will be

blessed? For I have loved him, because he commands
his children and his household after him that they keep
God's way, doing charity and justice. (Exod. 18:17–19)

Here God identifies faithfulness to the covenant with per-
formance of acts of charity and justice. And Abraham lives
up to God's expectations, even when the pursuit of justice
requires confronting God. When God makes Abraham
aware of the plan to destroy the sinful residents of Sodom
and Gomorrah, Abraham speaks out to God: "Will You also
wipe out the innocent along with the wicked? ... It would be
sacrilege for You to do so such a thing.... Shall the Judge of
all the earth not act justly?" (Gen. 18:23, 25).

When God concedes that all of Sodom will be spared
destruction if fifty righteous persons can be found there,
Abraham persists. On behalf of the innocent he pleads,
"Please behold that I desire to speak to my Lord, I who am
only dust and ashes" (Gen. 18:27). By describing himself as
"dust and ashes," words that Job will later use to underscore
his humility, Abraham calls attention to God's role as creator and to his own fleeting presence in the world. Abraham
chooses these words as he prepares to launch into a full-
fledged challenge to the Lord of the Universe, an act of ultimate chutzpah, of audacity intended to move God to do
justice and protect the righteous. Abraham continues his
negotiation on behalf of the righteous of Sodom until God
agrees, "I will not destroy for the sake of the ten" (Gen.
18:32). From Abraham we learn that to live in covenant, to
become a blessing, requires of us acts of compassion, justice,
and even audacity.

We see that to be a blessing is to perform simple acts of
kindness or to speak out against injustice. We too can draw
from our own experiences as wanderers and from our own
times of despair. We possess gifts of humility and compassion

that can bring great comfort into a world that feels dark and lonely. Like Abraham and Sarah from their tent, we can humbly offer comfort, serving as reminders of the goodness of the world—and thereby become a blessing. Like Abraham in his debate with God, we can demand justice, even on behalf of innocent strangers, fellow children of God. With acts of charity and justice, kindness and compassion, we become blessings.

I Was Often Hungry: Stories of Humility

Our own suffering, past or present, may bring us greater empathy and prompt us to respond with compassion. Rabbi Luria identified the human task as participation in the repair of the world by living a life of holiness. In a broken world, we live a life of repair when we live with compassion and thereby become a blessing to others. You may be a blessing to others without even being aware of your role by visiting the sick, listening to those in crisis, or offering a helping hand to someone in need.

I recall an incident from my childhood when my family was living in a rural area outside of Phoenix. We rarely had unexpected visitors. One day there was a knock at the door and I answered to find a disheveled man who could not speak. I had never seen anyone like him before and he frightened me. I ran to get my father, and the man pointed to his stomach. My father very politely and with a smile asked the stranger to wait by the door, went into the kitchen, and returned with a bag of food. My father offered the bag to the man, treating him with respect, and wished him well. As the man left, my

> You may be a blessing to others by visiting the sick, listening to those in crisis, or offering a helping hand to someone in need.

father turned to me as I stood by wide-eyed, and said, "When I was young, I was often terribly hungry. I know what it means to be without food. No one should have to suffer that way." My father, who had fended for himself in his adolescence and during World War II, had transformed his suffering into a blessing of compassion and kindness for others. In doing acts of holiness he became a blessing, and in becoming a blessing he found a way of restoring divine sparks to their source.

Our own darkest moments can become the source of a light, a blessing that we carry to others. An obstetrician from my congregation in recent years passed through the nightmare of treatment for mantle cell lymphoma, undergoing chemotherapy and a bone marrow transplant. Now in remission, this physician, who had always been known for his compassion, offers strangers who call him a message of hope, based on his firsthand knowledge that healing is possible. He reassures those fighting cancer that they too will find the strength to persevere despite the hardships.

> Our own darkest moments can become the source of a light, a blessing that we carry to others.

Our encounters with despair prepare us to be of service to others. I am reminded of two ministers I met through my work as a police chaplain, individuals who have struggled with alcoholism. Today, as recovering alcoholics with many years of sobriety, they are willing and able to counsel police officers struggling with drinking problems. Like Abraham, they welcome strangers who ask for their help. Like the obstetrician, they offer the profound insight, understanding, and care that come with firsthand experience of pain and recovery. These chaplains have healed, and out of gratitude for their recovery, they have chosen to make their suffering a blessing to others in despair—by listening, guiding, and offering their very presence as a demonstration of the goodness in the world.

Much of this book has dealt with my own story and ways in which my trauma of despair has made it possible for me to become a caregiver. From my memories of my utter hopelessness, I can enter into the darkness of a soul in pain. When I listen, I try to do so with attentiveness to the unspoken, and with a focus on honoring the gifts within the suffering soul. I am aware of the presence of divine sparks in each person, sparks that yearn to return to the Creator, to the source of goodness. I strive to convey hope. Even with healing, I still encounter anxiety— over my work, my relationships, my calling. I am reminded of the statement of the early Rabbis that in this world, unlike the world to come, there is no complete rejoicing.[2] In this world, joy is often alloyed with anxiety; achievement tinged by envy. I have recovered from my pervasive sense of despair. And yet there are souls for whom depression is chronic, for whom life's burdens create a constant, persistent heaviness. Even for those who continue to suffer, despair can become a source of perspective, strength, and ultimately blessing.

> Even for those who continue to suffer, despair can become a source of perspective, strength, and ultimately blessing.

To Bind Up the Nation's Wounds: Lincoln's Vision

Abraham Lincoln struggled throughout his life with chronic depression, and from his suffering he drew courage and wisdom. Joshua Wolf Shenk describes Abraham Lincoln's constant battle with depression in his work *Lincoln's Melancholy: How Depression Challenged a President and Fueled His Greatness*.[3] In 1860 in Decatur, Illinois, the state's Republican representatives had unanimously nominated Lincoln as their presidential candidate. He had been a surprise choice, having served only a single term as an Illinois congressman and having run unsuccessfully for the U.S. Senate. His oratory and debating skills, particularly on the topic of slavery, had propelled him onto the national stage as the "Rail-Splitter Candidate."

Schenk describes the aftermath of Lincoln's statewide victory in gaining the Illinois delegation's support as follows:

> The next day, the convention closed.... After the wigwam had emptied, the lieutenant governor of the state, William J. Bross, walked the floor. He noticed his state party's choice for president sitting alone at the end of the hall. Lincoln's head was bowed, his gangly arms bent at the elbows, his hands pressed to his face. As Bross approached, Lincoln noticed him and said, "I'm not very well." Lincoln's look at that moment—the classic image of gloom—was familiar to everyone who knew him well. These spells were common. And they were just a thread in a curious fabric of behavior and thought that Lincoln's friends and colleagues called his "melancholy."[4]

This melancholy would inform and inspire Lincoln throughout his lifetime. Lincoln's bouts of severe depression began when he was in his mid-twenties. After his friend Ann Rutledge died of typhoid, Lincoln withdrew from the company of friends and spoke of suicide. His friends volunteered in a suicide watch for several weeks and his depression persisted for months.[5]

A few years later, in the midst of a winter that followed a long period of intense work and fatigue, Lincoln suffered another emotional collapse. In his early thirties and not yet married, Lincoln emerged from his hard-fought battle against despair with a greater sense of clarity. He said to his best friend, Joshua Fry Speed, that he had an "irrepressible desire to accomplish something while he lived that would 'link his name with something that would redound to the interest of his fellow man.'"[6] In the next phase of his life, Lincoln married and worked diligently as a lawyer, then served as a congressman for one term, and lost a run for the U.S. Senate. Although depression plagued him, he developed strategies to move forward. He used humor to lift his spirits. He employed self-discipline to accomplish small daily acts despite turmoil and he looked at reality squarely, accepting its imperfection and difficulties, As the years progressed, he developed a deeper belief in divine providence. Lincoln's story is not a happily-ever-after tale in which he was cured of melancholia, but an illustration of how ongoing despair can be integrated into a life of purpose and meaning.

Lincoln employed the skills he had gained throughout his years of struggle with depression to guide the nation through the Civil War. He exposed false optimism and articulated a compelling vision of a free society, despite the recognition that it would be actualized imperfectly. Lincoln, in his wisdom rooted in a life of struggle, recognized that the world is broken and that souls are shattered. He demonstrated an unflappable tolerance for uncertainty, a willingness to move forward despite pain, and a capacity for crafting approaches to obstacles. During difficult times, he prayed and read scripture, particularly the Book of Job. When his friends said that they feared for his assassination, Lincoln replied, "God's will be done. I am in His hands."[7] As the war drew to a close, Lincoln was observed by his secretary of the interior, James Harlan:

> That indescribable sadness which had previously seemed to be an adamantine element of his very being, had been suddenly exchanged for an equally indescrib-

able expression of serene joy, as if conscious that the great purpose of his life had been achieved ... yet there was no manifestation of exaltation or ecstasy. He seemed the very personification of supreme satisfaction.[8]

Lincoln had fulfilled his sense of destiny, serving both his nation and his God. His greatness was clearly informed and shaped by his own inner battles. From his darkness emerged great insight, a tolerance for chaos, and the patience to move forward step-by-step, despite uncertainty, toward an overarching goal. These qualities guided our nation and would later help the nation to heal. At the end of the war, Lincoln demonstrated his extraordinary capacity for offering forgiveness and assuming responsibility. In his second inaugural address of March 4, 1864, when Northern victory was near at hand, he spoke of reconciliation. Lincoln argued that both the North and the South were responsible for American slavery. In the words of Joshua Wolf Schenk: "Lincoln knew the tendency of victors in a grueling conflict was to seek vengeance and of the vanquished to turn bitter. He argued that both sides should bear in mind their shared wrong and see their common opportunity."[9]

The concluding words of Lincoln's second inaugural address achieve the grandeur of biblical language:

With malice toward none, with charity for all; with firmness in the right, as God gives us to see the right, let us strive on to finish the work we are in; to bind up the nation's wounds; to care for him who shall have borne the battle, and for his widow and his orphan—to do all which may achieve and cherish a just and lasting peace among ourselves, and with all nations.

Here Lincoln asks that the nation be blessed and that her inhabitants become a blessing.

Today Lincoln is consistently chosen in surveys as the greatest of America's presidents, the man who—like Moses—guided our nation during its time of utmost crisis. The stakes in this crisis were the future of the United States and the outcome of a war in which more American lives would be lost than at any time in our nation's history before or since. For Lincoln, constant turmoil and the threat of chaos were realities he faced regularly in his inner life. Lincoln's steadfastness was a product of a lifetime of struggle and of his conscious decision to live a life of significance. His faith in his calling prepared him to persist in facing the awesome and awful decisions of a president leading a country in crisis.

The Black Dog of Despair: Churchill's Purpose from Struggle

Another historic leader whose greatness was fueled by a lifetime of struggle with despair is Winston Churchill. On May 10, 1940, on the eve of Germany's invasion of France, Neville Chamberlain resigned as Great Britain's prime minister, recognizing the failure of his policy of appeasement and acknowledging his lack of popular support. Winston Churchill was appointed prime minister by King George IV and also took on the office of minister of defense, guiding his nation throughout World War II. Churchill refused to negotiate with Germany or seek an armistice, despite growing political pressure to do so. He proclaimed, "Victory at all costs, victory in spite of all terror, victory however long and hard the road may be for without victory there is no survival." Churchill's steadfast strength in the face of overwhelming odds and his repeated moving oratory buoyed his nation and the Allied forces, bolstering the successful counterattacks against the Nazis from 1942 to 1945.

Throughout his life, Churchill suffered from bouts of depression.[10] In some cases, he wrote, "black dog" prevented him from getting out of bed. His nickname for his depression suited the lifelong companion whom he knew well and sought to master. A contemporary wrote of him: "What a creature of strange moods he is, always at the top of the wheel of confidence, or at the bottom of an intense depression."[11] In a biography of Churchill, William Manchester writes, "All his life he suffered spells of depression.... The deep reservoir of vehemence he carried within him backed up and he was plunged into fathomless gloom."[12] Yet it was that same intensity that allowed Churchill to serve as a formidable force on behalf of England and the Allies during World War II, calling for the offering of "blood, toil, tears, and sweat" against the armies of Hitler. Again, Manchester explains:

> His basic weakness became his basic strength. Here, at last, was pure evil, a monster who deserved no pity, a tyrant he could claw and maim without admonishment from his scruples. By provoking his titanic wrath, the challenge from central Europe released enormous stores of long-suppressed vitality within him.... He declared to Lord Moran: "This can not be accident, it must be designed. I was kept for this job."[13]

For Churchill, his inner rage and need for purpose were transformed in a time of international crisis into an unwavering focus on an evil foe, allowing him to lead in a time of hopelessness. His years of struggle with depression prepared him, like Lincoln before him, for his role in history.[14]

There Is Meaning: Buber's Presence

Lincoln and Churchill spent lifetimes battling despair and learning from their struggles, growing in inner strength to meet the extraordinary challenges of national survival, but others may encounter a single moment of crisis that gives birth to sudden insight and lifelong transformation. A traumatic event, once we own it and understand it, can awaken us to a new worldview and an opportunity to be a blessing. Martin Buber's encounter with a young man's suicide, for which he felt in part responsible, propelled him to create a philosophy of life that emphasized the importance of listening within an I-Thou relationship.

In his best-known work, *I and Thou*,[15] Martin Buber describes two kinds of relationships: I-It and I-Thou. I-Its are user relationships, which are not bad, just incomplete. When we relate to other people as objects, we engage in an I-It relationship, for example in dealing with a person who is performing a service for us, such as a waiter or taxi driver. We may relate to loved ones this way in tending to daily tasks. The I-It relationship is result-oriented. In I-Thou relationships, however, the interaction is the goal. In relating to another as a Thou, we appreciate the uniqueness of the other person and the moment. Buber would write that we encounter the divine when we engage others with our full presence.

> We encounter the divine when we engage others with our full presence.

Buber wrote of the experience that changed his worldview in his work *Between Man and Man*, under the heading "A Conversion":

> What happened was no more than that one forenoon, after a morning of "religious" enthusiasm, I had a visit from an unknown young man, without being there in spirit. I certainly did not fail to let the meeting be friendly, I did not treat him any more remissly than all his contemporaries who were in the habit of seeking me out about this time of day as an oracle that is ready to listen to reason. I conversed attentively and openly

with him—only I omitted to guess the questions which he did not put. Later, not long after, I learned from one of his friends—he himself was no longer alive—the essential content of these questions; I learned that he had come to me not casually, but borne by destiny, not for a chat but for a decision. He had come to me, he had come in this hour. What do we expect when we are in despair and yet go to a man? Surely a presence by means of which we are told that nevertheless there is meaning.[16]

Buber faulted himself for missing the subtext of the student's question. He would thereafter inspire others with his teaching on the importance of being fully attentive to another person, of the need to engage in I-Thou relationships.

I-It and I-Thou relationships in my own life exist on a continuum, at opposite ends of a spectrum. In a counseling setting, my goal is to be fully present for the person with whom I am meeting within an I-Thou context. I strive to understand the pain, to hear the unspoken, on all four levels: from the physical events to the emotional state, from the thought process to the intuitive sense of the meaning of the loss. Our presence can serve as a reminder to a soul in despair that kindness and purpose persist in this broken world.

There is something about every story of suicide that leaves us bewildered, vulnerable, and lost. In the case of Martin Buber's experience, he judged himself responsible at the critical juncture in the life of a young man. Yet Buber had not closed the door on the young man. He had been polite, but he had failed to hear the unspoken questions of purpose and meaning, to recognize the quiet desperation of a soul on the brink of the abyss. He had failed to be fully present for another person in need of kindness. Ultimately, the student was responsible for his own death, for choosing not to share his anguish and to receive a message of hope. Yet from hindsight, Buber realized that offering "meaning" is often a lifeline to a person who is suicidal.

Active listening can offer compassion by taking in a story without passing judgment, by responding to the unspoken questions, and by addressing the questions of identity and purpose. And more, Buber recognized that we find the divine not in the moment of the ecstatic experience alone, but in the simple, daily task of being fully present with others and thereby with God. Out of the pain of loss, Buber crafted an identity and chose a worldview that profoundly influenced his readers. His message was to create divine moments through day-to-day encounters with fellow souls. Buber—like Abraham, like my father, like the obstetrician, like the chaplains—found that suffering brought with it the gifts of humility and compassion, sources we draw on in order to become a blessing.

A Sacred Act of Kindness: Listening

Martin Buber's story is a reminder of the enormous responsibility of listening to a soul in pain. On the one hand, most of us are not able to assess the depth and gravity of a soul's pain and to respond appropriately. On the other hand, I recall studies conducted on the efficacy of counseling that indicate that the single factor most directly correlated with sufferers' perceived improvement was whether they believed that their counselors had genuinely cared about their well-being.[17] To listen to another person is to bring comfort through connection. There is a statement in the Talmud that when you visit a person who is physically ill, you take away one-sixtieth of the pain.[18] In listening to a soul in pain, sometimes all we can offer is mindful listening. And in that act of listening, we validate that the soul is worthy of time and attention, that the burdens that cause the pain are real and heavy, and that good continues to exist in a broken world. Our very presence as caring listeners attests to the kindness that exists in an imperfect but beautiful world.

Again, let me offer a caution in knowing our own limits as listeners. I once asked Dr. Abraham Twerski, "How do you do your work as a therapist day in and day out and protect yourself?" He just smiled and said, "If you really care, you will feel another's pain, and if you feel another's pain, it will take its toll." Dr. Twerski, who struggled to find his calling, ultimately decided after completing his rabbinic ordination to embark on medical school studies. In dedicating his life to working with individuals suffering from addictions, he seeks the divine sparks within tortured souls. In serving patients from all walks of life with humility and understanding, he makes the ideal of I-Thou relationships a reality. In crafting dozens of works on the subject of healing, he offers compassion and a willingness to advocate for those suffering.

> Our very presence as caring listeners attests to the kindness that exists in an imperfect but beautiful world.

The challenge in listening, whether in the context of family relationships or friendships, the workplace or everyday interactions, is twofold. First, stories of pain make the empathetic listener feel great sorrow. Second, listening to souls immersed and even stuck in their own struggles, unwilling to consider paths to healing, is frustrating work. The frustration comes with the realization that the speaker is resisting change, and that without change the pain will persist. Sadly, those most in need of professional help or a shift in perspective are often the least willing to acknowledge those needs. Listening without judging or commenting to someone stuck in the same place is exhausting. In order to continue to be a caring presence, we must set reasonable limits. It is obvious that if we were to listen to one story of pain endlessly, we would be exceeding any reasonable expectations. We require limits on our time and energies devoted to listening because we must care for ourselves in order to care for others. Resources devoted to someone who is not finding comfort is also time taken away from someone else who is seeking hope. And yet whenever we listen to a suffering soul, we offer a precious gift and in doing so we become a blessing.

To Look to the Future:
The Dalai Lama's Insight

In counseling, particularly counseling that is spiritually based, there is a need to offer the speaker the opportunity to craft future chapters of a life story. In meetings of Alcoholics Anonymous, this drafting of a life story often begins: "Hi, my name is Dan and I'm an alcoholic." The telling of a life story places the dark past within the context of a larger whole, a life marked by gratitude for the present and hope for the future. For the Jewish people, our belief in a future has allowed us to survive in the darkest times. As we conclude the retelling of our Exodus from Egypt each Passover, we declare, "Next year in Jerusalem." Jerusalem represents the hope of a dispersed and persecuted people to gather in the land God described to Abraham. And more, we are reminded that God told Abraham that in the land, he would become a blessing. Since the creation of the State of Israel in 1948, the declaration "Next year in Jerusalem" refers to our ancient yearning to live in covenant with God in a healed world.

Depression is often identified as hopelessness, the sense that life is going nowhere. Healing comes with crafting future chapters of our life story, chapters in which despair may become the source of humility, compassion, and gratitude. Viktor Frankl, a psychotherapist who survived the Nazi death camps, reflected after the war that many survivors found the will to survive by foreseeing chapters to come in the stories of their lives. These chapters told stories of reuniting with loved ones, or in his case, rewriting a destroyed book.[19] As we heal, we draft new chapters—one page at a time—and with new chapters comes the possibility of purpose.

The significance of a story with a grand future purpose was beautifully explained by the Dalai Lama. More than twenty years ago, the Dalai Lama invited a group of Jewish scholars to visit with him in Dharamsala, India. As the leader of a people exiled from its homeland, he was curious to understand how the Jews had maintained their identity during two thousand years of exile. In response, one scholar described the annual Passover seder. Another scholar emphasized that the Jewish community relied upon the Shabbat, the weekly day of rest inspired by God's pause from the work of creation. A third suggested that *kashrut*, the dietary laws, remind us every time we eat that we are a people with shared rituals and principles. The Dalai Lama listened and with his signature grin responded that the Jewish people have survived because they believe that God has chosen them for a specific purpose. He maintained that a people does not survive only by clinging to their past or living in the present, but by looking with purpose to the future. The Dalai Lama proposed that the Jews' belief that God has called them to be a light unto the nations had been the key to Jewish survival.[20] The covenant, which calls upon the

> As we heal, we draft new chapters and with new chapters comes the possibility of purpose.

Israelites to do what is just and right, presents a purpose, a future, and the hope of becoming a blessing.

Faith in the Destination: Moses's Work of Repair

What did covenant mean to Moses, who would witness God's revelation at Mount Sinai, transforming the covenant from a relationship between God and a small clan into a commitment to God by an entire people? How do we live in covenant in our own time, performing deeds that allow us to be a blessing? Defining *covenant* is difficult, because the term keeps appearing in different contexts in the unfolding of the Torah. To better understand the duties and nature of covenant, we turn to the Torah beginning with a reference to covenant that appears in the story of Noah.

God initially speaks to Noah of covenant only in passing, "But I will keep My covenant with you and you shall enter the ark" (Gen. 6:18). Soon after, God reveals more about why Noah was chosen to be a partner in God's covenant, "Go into the ark … for you alone have I found righteous before Me in this generation" (Gen. 7:1). After the flood in the story of Noah, God establishes a covenant with the whole of creation, symbolized by the rainbow and the unilateral promise never again to destroy creation (Gen. 9:8–17).

Ten generations later, God calls to Abraham, "go forth … to the land that I will show you … and you shall become a blessing" (Gen. 12:1–2). After settling in the land, God pledges that Abraham's descendants will inherit the land (Gen. 15:8). Later, God will further clarify the acts of loyalty owed by both parties to this sacred covenant. After twenty-four years in the land, when Abraham is already ninety-nine years old, God will state that because Abraham and his descendants are identified with acts of justice and righteousness, God will in turn make them a great nation in the land (Gen. 18:19). God will later affirm in speaking to Abraham's son Isaac, that the covenant endures and that Isaac and his descendants too shall be a blessing to all the inhabitants of the land "in as much as Abraham obeyed Me and kept My charge, My commandments, my decrees, and my laws" (Gen. 26:5). The covenant with Abraham is different than God's covenant with Noah. God has expectations of Abraham and his descendants, specifically that they live righteously, unlike the pledge made to Noah that was unconditional.

In the course of Abraham's story, God presents only a few explicit commandments that are recorded in the text. After Moses ascends Mount Sinai, God delivers comprehensive legislation, beginning with the Ten Commandments. The laws inscribed on the two stone tablets and their elaboration through subsequent commands will offer guidance for living according to God's ways. Just before the revelation at Mount Sinai, God had asked Moses to convey to the Israelites an offer: if the people will observe the covenant, they will be a "kingdom of priests and a holy nation to Me" (Exod. 19:5). The Israelites responded, "all that God has spoken we will do" (Exod. 19:8). As in the case of Abraham, the covenant at Sinai was an agreement by both sides. In this case, the big change is that the covenant is made between God and an entire people, and the covenant sets forth explicit laws for the people to follow. The Israelites entered into a commitment to partner with God in the work of healing the world by living justly, righteously, and faithfully. In our own lives, we too are called to live with a commitment to perform acts of charity and justice, with the assurance that in time our purpose will be revealed.

When God had his first conversation with the shepherd Moses at the burning bush, God made a promise: "I have indeed seen the suffering of My people that is in Egypt.... I will bring them out of the land to a good and spacious land, to a land flowing with milk and honey" (Exod. 3:8). God understood that in order for the people to emerge from Egypt, the narrow place, from the rut of generations of servitude, from a history devoid of will, the Israelites would need a vision for the future. That vision gave the people a direction, a purpose, a story that would unfold in chapters that were unimaginable when they were enslaved in Egypt. This promise of a land of milk and honey, a place of freedom, is repeated at least fifteen times in the Torah during the era of Moses's leadership. The significance of the Exodus story for the Jewish people is that we can choose hope in times of despair, that the Promised Land awaited us even while we were slaves in Egypt, that liberation would become the reality of an enslaved people.

When leaving Egypt, the Israelites were filled with anxiety. Like many of us, they found transitions and changes were hard, even coming from the misery of their lives as slaves. Just six weeks after departing from Egypt, the Israelites groaned to Moses, "If only we had died by God's hand in Egypt. There at least we could sit by pots of meat and eat our fill of bread, but you had to bring us out to this desert to kill the entire community by starvation" (Exod. 16:3). Even after liberation from slavery, after the passage from Egypt to the desert, the Israelites faced uncertainty and hardships every day of the journey through the desert. In our own lives, periods of change are fraught with uncertainty and a yearning for the familiar, even when the familiar is painful. The entire journey through the desert would prove difficult, marked by bouts of despair, both for the people and for God. And yet, faith in the destination, in the ending to the story of wandering, in a home in the land God promised to Abraham, gave the people a sense of purpose and of becoming a blessing.

God's Despair: Regretting Creation

Despair is present in the lives of heroes and healers great and small, from the leader Moses to the strudel baker of the folktale in chapter 1. In the Torah we find that even God encounters despair, time and again. When we read the Bible text closely, we discover a new dimension of God, a God in crisis who models for us healing by heeding a message, recrafting identity, and choosing to see the creation as good. In so doing, God heals from anger and finds renewed purpose. We use the Hebrew text to gain insights into this God of despair and hope.

God, from the very beginning of the Torah, yearns for relationship with humankind but is repeatedly disappointed. In the words of Jerusalem philosopher Rabbi David Hartman, "The most emotional and developed personality in the Torah is God."[21] As God's character unfolds, we find God betrayed by humankind and suffering utter despair. Consider the story of creation. In chapter 1 of Genesis, creation unfolds as an orderly process and at the close of each day (except day two), God surveys creation and "God saw that it was good." On the sixth day, we are reminded four times in Genesis 1:26–27 that God fashioned humanity in the image of God, a reminder of the capacity for creativity, choice, and good within each soul. At the close of that sixth day of creation, God reviews creation and proclaims, "And behold, it was *very* good." And yet, by chapter 6 of Genesis, God has already fallen from the heights of joy to the depths of despair. In these chapters ten generations have come and gone: Eve and Adam have violated the single rule God presented to them and have been banished; Cain has murdered his brother; and there is a vague description of widespread sexual carnality. God despairs:

> God saw that human wickedness on earth was increasing…. God regretted making humanity on earth and

was pained to the very core. God said, "I will obliterate humanity that I have created from the face of the earth—people, livestock, land animals, and the birds of the sky. I regret that I created them." (Gen. 6:5–7)

Since the world is an extension of God, these words signify God's alienation from creation and a desire to destroy much of the creation.

God's words and works have turned to evil and God wishes to blot out all the living beings. God's anger erupts from hopelessness, from betrayal, and from pain. This despair reminds us of Rachel, Moses, and Job, who found they could not go on. Yet here in this moment, on the brink of the obliteration of humankind, there is a pause in the text, a moment in which God reappraises the destructive impulse. The text quickly offers a new frame of reference, a new hope. The next line reads "But Noah found grace in God's eyes." The name *Noah* means "comfort."[22] The center word of the five-word Hebrew phrase is *grace*, an overflowing of kindness. On the verge of destroying creation, God shifts perspective: God heeds the message of Noah's presence, is reminded of God's identity as creator, and reclaims a worldview of grace. The contemporary Jerusalem Bible scholar Avivah Zornberg describes the importance of seeing in this scene: "God declares an intention, based on a vision, and immediately revokes it, because of another vision of things."[23] We learn from God's example that a changed worldview may offer hope and healing.

> We learn from God's example that a changed worldview may offer hope and healing.

Noah is a redemptive blessing: a man of integrity in his generation, evidence that good exists in a broken world. In looking at Noah, God pauses and looks again at creation, and overcomes despair and anger. In looking at Noah, God finds a single good point of creation, and (as Rebbe Nachman counseled) that single, good point allows for a shift in perspective. God resolves to move beyond anger, to be inspired by Noah's grace to start the creation story over, this time with a righteous individual and his family. Noah serves as a blessing to God, prompting God to pause, look again, and find a message of hope. We in turn are inspired to live in such a way as to serve as a blessing.

God's Rage: The Israelites and the Golden Calf

Moving forward from Genesis chapter 6 to Exodus chapter 19, we find that God has delivered the descendents of Abraham and Sarah from servitude in Egypt through the Red Sea to the Sinai desert. After two months in the desert, Moses ascends to Mount Sinai where God affirms the covenant originally made with Abraham. At Mount Sinai God sends a message to the people through Moses: "You have seen what I did to Egypt, and that I have borne you on the wings of eagles and brought you to Me. And now, if you obey Me and observe My covenant, you shall be to Me the most beloved treasure of all peoples.... You will be a kingdom of priests and a holy nation unto Me" (Exod. 19:4–6). These are words that describe an enduring, covenantal relationship with the Israelite people.

After the people tell Moses, "Everything that the Lord has spoken we shall do!" (Exod. 19:8), God is prepared to descend "in the sight of the entire people on Mount Sinai" (Exod. 19:11). God's hope is that the Israelites will follow the commandments, serving as a model of faithfulness for other nations. In exchange, God promises companionship, direction, and protection. At this pivotal moment in Jewish history, the scene is described with great drama: the people stand at the foot of Mount Sinai, which is ablaze in flames, issuing smoke, and quaking. The Israelites pledge to heed the divine message by following God's commands.[24] Freedom is the ability to choose our commitments. It is our commitments that define who we are and offer us purpose.

And yet here, too, God will find that the world is never fully fixed and that the work of repair is ongoing. God invites Moses up to the top of the mountain to receive the symbolic tablets upon which divine words were engraved to offer guidance for living the covenant. While Moses spends forty days on Mount Sinai, the Israelites begin to panic. They demand of Moses's brother Aaron, "Make for us a god to lead us. We have no idea what happened to Moses, the man who brought us out of Egypt" (Exod. 32:1). With Aaron's help they fashion a golden calf, a god to whom they bring offerings and before whom they celebrate. God's covenant requires faithfulness to God, God's laws, and acting right-eously. God reveals to Moses the people's idolatry, their dis-loyalty to their covenantal oath, their corruption. God commands Moses, "Go down—for the people whom you brought out from Egypt have become corrupt.... I have observed the people and they are a defiant people. Do not try to stop Me when I unleash my rage against them to oblit-erate them. I will then make you Moses into a great nation" (Exod. 32:7–9). Only forty days after entering into covenant at Sinai, God sees the people of the covenant engaged in infi-delity and responds with a familiar impulse to destroy.[25]

At this point God restates to Moses the promise made to Abraham, that "I will make of you a great nation." The pat-tern established with Noah is repeated: God loses hope in humanity and threatens to begin all over again with a single

> It is our commitments that define who we are and offer us purpose.

soul. Yet God, in expressing anger aloud, reframes and begins to heal.[26]

Moses immediately shifts the responsibility for the people to God, saying "*Your* people whom *You* have taken out of the land of Egypt." Moses reminds God that the exodus was a product of "great power and a strong hand," a feat of great commitment. Moses prompts God to reconsider with the argument: "Why should Egypt be able to say that You took them [the Israelites] out with evil intentions, to kill them in the hill country, and wipe them out from the face of the earth?" (Exod. 32:12). Moses appeals to God to remember the covenant, asking God to remain faithful: "Remember Your servants, Abraham, Isaac, and Jacob. You swore to them by Your very essence and declared that You would make their descendents as numerous as the stars of the sky, giving their descendents the land You promised so that they would be able to occupy it forever" (Exod. 32:13). Moses does not excuse the people's wrongdoing, but he appeals to God's qualities of divine goodness and faithfulness.

In response to Moses's plea, God pardons, but does not fully forgive.[27] At first God is not prepared to accompany the Israelites through the desert, to fully reconcile with them. Only after Moses spends another forty days and forty nights atop Mount Sinai to plead for forgiveness, and the people remain faithful throughout his absence, does God accept their repentance and renew the relationship with the Israelites. Maimonides wrote that repentance means to be in the same situation in which you have periodically failed but to remain true to the course with steadfast restraint.[28] The symbol of forgiveness from God to humankind is a newly crafted set of stone tablets bearing the Ten Commandments.

As Moses prepares to descend from Mount Sinai with the new set of tablets, he makes an additional request: "Please let me have a vision of Your Glory" (Exod. 33:18). In response,

God offers a proclamation that begins: "The Ever-Present-One, a God compassionate and gracious, slow to anger, and abundant in kindness and truth" (Exod. 34:6). It is as if God sings these words with pride for the recently revealed capacity for forgiveness. God is learning that to reclaim relationship and maintain covenant requires accepting and forgiving the people for their frailties. Just as God in the Bible learns from crisis, so we are challenged to find hope amid despair, to seek understanding and offer forgiveness.

God's Forgiveness: The Report from Canaan

In Numbers, chapters 13 and 14, God is once again severely tested by the Israelites. This story of betrayal will not end in a pardon. The tale begins when God commands Moses to send emissaries to Canaan to bring back a report on the territory. When the twelve leaders, one from each tribe, return after forty days, they all confirm that it is a land flowing with milk and honey. Yet ten of the spies warn that the people who inhabit the land are far too mighty to be conquered. The Israelites, succumbing to fear, weep and cry out, "If only we had died in the land of Egypt, or if only we had died in this wilderness! Why is God bringing us to this land to die by the sword?... Is it not better for us to return to Egypt?" (Num. 14:2–3). Only two of the emissaries, Joshua and Caleb, declare, "the land is very, very good!... do not fear.... The Ever-Present-One is with us" (Num. 14:8–9). These words of faith not only fail to persuade, they even inflame the people.

When the people are on the verge of entering into the Promised Land, fulfilling the promise made by God to Abraham, they renounce their faith in God. They conspire against God, saying to one another, "Let us appoint a leader and let us return to Egypt" (Num. 14:4). God speaks to

Moses with bitterness: "How long will this people provoke Me, and how long will they not have faith in Me, despite all the signs that I have performed in their midst? I will smite them with the plague and annihilate them, and I shall make you a greater and more powerful nation than they" (Num. 14:11–12). Once again betrayed, God despairs, rages, and plans to destroy. Moses uses his old tactics from the golden calf episode, arguing that Egypt and other nations will accuse God of breaking the covenantal promise and lacking the power to bring the people to the land.

In addressing God, Moses revises the words of self-description God spoke at Sinai in Exodus 34:6, now emphasizing God's patience and kindness.[29] God responds to Moses's forceful plea: "I will grant forgiveness as you have requested" (Num. 14:20). And then, as if in the same breath, God qualifies the statement: Those who betrayed me shall perish in the desert; only their children, along with Caleb, Joshua, and their families, shall enter the Promised Land. In the words of Abraham Joshua Heschel: "One must not mistake divine forgiveness for indulgence or complacency. There is a limit at which forbearance ceases to be a blessing. Forgiveness is neither absolute nor unconditional."[30]

The Israelites' betrayal of the covenant does not derail the journey with the destination of the Promised Land, but it does change who will enter and when. God will continue to guide the people in a cloud by day and a fire by night, but the relationship is forever altered. In the analysis of Maimonides: "One cannot be expected to leave the state of slavery, toiling in bricks and straw, and go to fight with giants. It was therefore a part of the divine wisdom to make them wander through the wilderness until they had become schooled in courage, until a new generation had grown up who had never known humiliation and bondage."[31] God continues to learn from despair, seeking to understand the

Israelites' fear and to remain faithful to the ultimate promises of the covenant.

How to Become a Blessing

The surprise of the Bible is not that God is described in
human terms as a corporeal God who took the people out of
Egypt with "a mighty hand and an outstretched arm," or who
warned Moses, "no human can see My face" (Exod. 33:20).
The surprise is that God's emotions are also described in
human terms. God despairs, God heals, and then God
despairs again. In the words of the sages, "The Torah is written in the words of humans."[32] In studying the Torah's
descriptions of God's despair and healing, we find insights
for our own lives. God shows us how to respond to despair:
articulating pain, pausing before acting, hearing a message of
hope, crafting an identity of mercy and compassion, choosing to see the world as good, and going on to become a blessing. God in our tradition models heroic healing.

These descriptions of God are surprising, because most
of us were taught that God is all knowing and perfect. Yet
here is a God that longs for relationship, as defined by the
covenant, only to experience pain and choose reconciliation.
In my counseling, I often ask those dealing with despair to
write a letter to God, to write as if God were the recipient.
The letters are composed with honesty, because we expect
that God knows us and our secrets. This conversation elicits
clarity and catharsis, which is the nature of heartfelt prayer.
I then ask the writers to respond to their letters as if they
were God. Responding from God's vantage point signifies
divine empathy. I find that the responses "from God" offer
direction, love, and acceptance.

Our process of healing ourselves and others begins with
acknowledging that we are shattered vessels that contain
divine sparks. To become a blessing, to offer compassion and

hope and healing, we must begin with humility. The word *blessing* in Hebrew, *brachah*, has a three-letter root that also appears in the word *birkayim* for knees and *breichah*, meaning a pool of water.[33] To be a blessing is to come before God in humility, upon our knees, aware of our own vulnerability and our own flaws. To be a blessing is to accept with gratitude that creation, as represented by a pool of water, is beyond our comprehension and contains an abundance of goodness. A blessing is a humble prayer to God asking God to bestow the abundance of life upon our loved ones.

To see the world through God's eyes in the biblical tradition is to acknowledge that the world is at once broken and good. God saw the good in creation on six successive days and saw the corruption of that creation on repeated occasions. Each time God encountered betrayal, God despaired, paused to see the world with grace and hope, then forgave. As God heeded the message of hope from Abraham, Noah, and Moses, so we must remain open to a message of healing. As God forgave the people after the episode of the golden calf for their infidelity, so we are called to forgive those who have hurt us. As God on seeing Noah accepted humanity despite corruption, so we must accept that brokenness exists alongside profound kindness. As God chose not to act from blind anger on hearing the report of the emissaries, but recognized the fears and limitations of the people, so we must move past anger toward understanding and healing. Forgiveness is not the denial of a wrong done, but an understanding and acceptance of the source of the wrong and the willingness to reclaim relationship. Forgiving ourselves means recognizing our capacity for the work of repair. To forgive is to unload weights that burden us and to proclaim that we who are created in God's image can become a blessing.

We are called upon to be a blessing. To be a blessing is God's promise to Abraham, to the people at Mount Sinai, and beyond. To be a blessing is a challenge and a duty, for all peoples. We are to look to God as the source of our inner, sacred sparks and we are to collect those sparks by imitating God's goodness. In Deuteronomy 11:22, God instructs the people to follow all of the commandments, walking in God's ways and cleaving to God. The Rabbis comment as follows on the call to walk in God's ways: "These are the ways of the Holy One.... [T]his means that just as God is gracious and compassionate, you too must be gracious and compassionate."³⁴

Losses impose heavy burdens upon us. Under the weight of the burdens we may find ourselves in a deep, dark, lonely place. This book has been about the experience of loss when it becomes utterly overwhelming. This book tells how, amid the shattered bits of our broken selves, we can uncover divine sparks, and with them bring light to others. This book acknowledges that even in the grip of suffering we can choose: choose to listen to the message of hope, choose to craft our identity, choose to accept a worldview of faith in the good in the world, and choose to discover our calling in healing the world. As Moses told the people, we are reminded: "You shall not corrupt the judgment of a proselyte or orphan, you shall not take the garment of a widow as a pledge. You shall remember that you were a slave in Egypt, and the Ever-Present-One, your God, redeemed you from there, therefore I command you to do this thing" (Deut. 24:17). We can choose to make the experience of pain a crucible of compassion for the needy and of humility in serving the most vulnerable.

> We can choose to make pain a crucible of compassion for the needy and of humility in serving the most vulnerable.

As shattered vessels we hold fast to shards that can reflect the light of a good world into the dark corners of souls in despair. Our experiences in a place of darkness leave us forever changed, mindful of the comfort a listener can bring. Our time spent suffering teaches us that a thoughtful listener can lighten the burdens that overwhelm us. Our own moments of pain show us that a caring listener is a blessing. Through our own despair we may become a source of comfort and hope to others. In the words of *The Big Book of Alcoholics Anonymous*, this simple but paradoxical truth is expressed as follows:

> Showing others who suffer how we were given help is the very thing which makes life seem so worthwhile to us now. Cling to the thought that, in God's hands, the dark past is the greatest possession you have—the key to life and happiness for others. With it you can avert death and misery for them.[35]

Although the world in which we live is broken, we have every reason to say, "It is good." And more, to do good, to live a life that is more whole and responds to God's call to live a life that is holy. Like Abraham the wanderer we can serve others with humility. Like Lincoln we can draw strength from our suffering and learn forgiveness from our despair. Like Churchill we can choose to make our pain a source of strength. Like Buber we can strive to listen for the unspoken. Like Dr. Abraham Twerski we can give of ourselves by honoring the divine in each person. Like Moses we can speak out in pursuit of justice. We are called to imitate God, to return again and again from hopelessness to hope, to see the world in all its brokenness filled with divine sparks. We are called to be a blessing: to alleviate suffering and to craft relationships grounded in love. And when we undertake the work of healing the world, we can look back on despair and look out on creation and echo God's words, "It is good."

Just as I summarized the Introduction with a prayer, so now, I conclude this book with the following words:

> *Rebono shel ha'olam*, source of mystery and presence, in this broken and beautiful world grant us the wisdom and strength to draw on our despair to do Your work, the work of repairing brokenness, collecting divine sparks, and healing the pain of souls, bit by bit. May we echo Your words, imitate Your deeds, and serve as a blessing on Your behalf. Amen.

Tools for Becoming a Blessing

Address Healing on Four Levels

To transform the pain surrounding a crisis, whether due to a loss, a betrayal, or a break-up, journal using the following four levels:

> *Pshat* (action/doing). What led to the crisis?
>
> *Remez* (emotion). What emotions evoked the event and do those emotions persist?
>
> *Drash* (intellect). How do you understand why this crisis occurred? What are the resources that could help you understand and heal?
>
> *Sod* (intuition).What did the crisis teach you? How did it make you better as a person? In what ways are there new beginnings that may emerge from the crisis?

Identify Your Distinctive Calling by Journaling

Journal: What are your strengths? What are your passions? What is a moment of trauma that you would wish to protect others from and a moment of rejoicing that you would like to enable others to experience? What is one small deed that you could do to help another? How and when will you do so? What is a grander plan for making a difference in the world that utilizes your strengths and resources? What is an act of goodness for others that you are already doing? What is a small step forward, an additional act of care that you are prepared to take now?

Practical Guidance Distilled: Checklists for Specific Areas of Concern

The following pages contain short checklists for those confronting despair. They can be used as a practical guide to beginning the healing process. Each checklist is designed to offer guidance for people facing specific challenges. These checklists are not meant to replace professional psychological care.

If you are feeling anxious without a clearly identifiable source

Know that anxiety in daily life is normal, a natural undertow amid life's waves. Yet, it is worth addressing on an ongoing basis to reduce its impact and enable greater joy and spontaneity. If the anxiety is a source of discomfort and distraction, consider moving through the following checklist.

❏ Get a physical exam by a doctor.

❏ Get enough sleep and eat wisely. Modest exercise, even a short walk, is a place to begin.

❏ Engage in enjoyable activities: listening to music, dancing, meditating, conversing with friends.

❏ Invite an old friend out for a cup of coffee or make a new friend.

❏ Schedule an appointment with a caring therapist.

❏ Write a letter "to God." Read the letter and then write to yourself spontaneously, as if God were responding to your letter.

❏ Set short- and long-term goals that are attainable.

❏ Consider a plan of action of caregiving to others in order to become a blessing.

This material is from *Healing from Despair: Choosing Wholeness in a Broken World* by Rabbi Elie Kaplan Spitz © 2008, published by Jewish Lights Publishing, P.O. Box 237, Woodstock, VT 05091. (802) 457-4000; www.jewishlights.com. The Publisher grants permission to you to copy this handout. All rights to other parts of this book are still covered by copyright and are reserved to the Publisher. Any other copying or usage requires written permission.

If your anxiety is due to the loss of health, a relationship, or a job

❑ Acknowledge that loss of health, a relationship, or a job has all the same rhythms as the loss of a loved one: denial, followed by anger, bargaining, depression, and (hopefully) acceptance. These stages don't necessarily move in a straight line and you may find yourself in the course of a single day moving between them. Give yourself time to get reoriented before moving forward.

❑ Examine what you learned from the situation, gaining the insight, humility, and gratitude that emerge from viewing the past.

❑ Forgive yourself with the recognition that you now have information and clarity that you lacked earlier when in the midst of your decision making.

❑ Make a plan to effect a change, envisioning your goals and the steps you would need to achieve the desired outcome. Break those necessary steps down into small increments and take the first step of action.

❑ Consider whether you are engaging in destructive behavior, such as self-medication with alcohol or drugs. Get physician guidance. If it feels like you can't live without the substance, you may have a problem of addiction. Consider supplementing the work with a therapist with an AA-type group, which may be found online at www.AlcoholicAnonymousMeeting.com.

This material is from *Healing from Despair: Choosing Wholeness in a Broken World* by Rabbi Elie Kaplan Spitz © 2008, published by Jewish Lights Publishing, P.O. Box 237, Woodstock, VT 05091. (802) 457-4000; www.jewishlights.com. The Publisher grants permission to you to copy this handout. All rights to other parts of this book are still covered by copyright and are reserved to the Publisher. Any other copying or usage requires written permission.

If you are grieving the loss of a loved one

❏ Allow time to process loss, knowing that you cannot control the timetable of acceptance and integration.

❏ Be gentle with yourself, accepting an initial reduction in attention span, energy, and patience. See yourself riding the waves of emotion that flow through you, allowing yourself to humbly feel the emotions and speak of them honestly.

❏ Actively process your grief, including speaking with caring listeners about memories of your loved one and what the loss means to you.

❏ Identify lessons learned from your loved one as a way to honor his or her goodness and legacy in order to integrate the best of who he or she was within yourself.

❏ Write a letter of farewell to your loved one—you may wish to place it in the grave if written before the funeral. Identify sources of gratitude to that person, and if there are areas of pain, address those too. Write a response as if your loved one was responding. After the letter exchange, write an additional letter to your loved one, offering compassionate forgiveness and acceptance, as well as gratitude.

❏ If you are part of a religious community, attend services to find comfort in belonging and continuity.

❏ Engage in honoring the deceased through the set rituals of your religious tradition.

This material is from *Healing from Despair: Choosing Wholeness in a Broken World* by Rabbi Elie Kaplan Spitz © 2008, published by Jewish Lights Publishing, P.O. Box 237, Woodstock, VT 05091. (802) 457-4000; www.jewishlights.com. The Publisher grants permission to you to copy this handout. All rights to other parts of this book are still covered by copyright and are reserved to the Publisher. Any other copying or usage requires written permission.

If you are grieving loss by a suicide

❏ Actively process the loss, because it is essential to healing.

❏ Speak with a therapist or clergy person whose professional training and experience support processing.

❏ Seek out a support group of other survivors of suicide. Those who have been in the same place have an insider's understanding and acceptance and can offer the hope of moving forward with life.

❏ Forgive yourself for not having prevented the suicide. Suicide is largely a compulsive act and once a person has decided to take his or her life and the decision is hidden, there is not much anyone can do to stop the final deed.

❏ Forgive the person who has taken his or her life. Feeling trapped and in excruciating pain prompted the irrational act.

❏ Reclaim a relationship with the deceased by embracing the good acts he or she performed before becoming clouded by despair. Your loved one was the person you knew and at times a stranger driven by compulsive behavior. Both are worth embracing compassionately.

❏ Extract memories of your loved one worth honoring.

This material is from *Healing from Despair: Choosing Wholeness in a Broken World* by Rabbi Elie Kaplan Spitz © 2008, published by Jewish Lights Publishing, P.O. Box 237, Woodstock, VT 05091. (802) 457-4000; www.jewishlights.com. The Publisher grants permission to you to copy this handout. All rights to other parts of this book are still covered by copyright and are reserved to the Publisher. Any other copying or usage requires written permission.

If you are feeling suicidal

❑ Get help. Go to a mental health professional. Tell a trusted friend. Call a hot line for support. The **National Suicide Prevention Lifeline** is a twenty-four-hour, toll-free suicide prevention service available to anyone in suicidal crisis. **If you need help, please dial 1-800-273-TALK (8255)**, or the National Hopeline Network, 1-800-SUICIDE (784-2433).

❑ Know that when people go through tough emotional times, the thought may arise, "I wish I were dead." It does not mean that you are crazy or bad for having the thought. Once you feel better, the thought will pass. If the thought is present and you are in emotional pain, find help. Know that the sooner you address the thought, the more easily the underlying problems can be addressed. If the thought feels strong, know that taking your own life does not solve the problems and will impose enormous pain on others. Do not cause your loved ones that pain.

❑ Know that there is reason to feel hope. The pain of despair usually passes. There are possibilities for change. There are people who love you. Know that you may have a biochemical imbalance that can be fixed. New pharmaceutical treatments and safer and more effective use of former treatments, such as electroconvulsive therapy, can realign your brain chemistry and enable you to feel good again.

❑ Know that it takes time to realign chemically and to reorient emotionally, mentally, and spiritually. Be gentle with yourself.

This material is from *Healing from Despair: Choosing Wholeness in a Broken World* by Rabbi Elie Kaplan Spitz © 2008, published by Jewish Lights Publishing, P.O. Box 237, Woodstock, VT 05091. (802) 457-4000; www.jewishlights.com. The Publisher grants permission to you to copy this handout. All rights to other parts of this book are still covered by copyright and are reserved to the Publisher. Any other copying or usage requires written permission.

If you have a friend who has suicidal thoughts

A professional best evaluates the seriousness of suicidal thoughts. Listen nonjudgmentally and compassionately and then encourage your friend to accept help from a mental health professional. If you have any concern that your friend may be imminently suicidal, call 911, the police, or take your friend to the emergency room. A friend may respond angrily to your "meddling." But it is wise to act and even to *over-react, because a life is at stake.*

This material is from *Healing from Despair: Choosing Wholeness in a Broken World* by Rabbi Elie Kaplan Spitz © 2008, published by Jewish Lights Publishing, P.O. Box 237, Woodstock, VT 05091. (802) 457-4000; www.jewishlights.com. The Publisher grants permission to you to copy this handout. All rights to other parts of this book are still covered by copyright and are reserved to the Publisher. Any other copying or usage requires written permission.

Notes

Introduction

1. My use of the word *spirituality* to mean "that which is uniquely human" is influenced by the writings of Dr. Abraham Twerski. See his *Twerski on Spirituality* (New York: Mesorah Publications, 1998). I am also reminded of the song of Disney's Jiminy Cricket, "You are a human animal; you are a very special breed. For you are the only animal who can think, who can reason, who can read." For a recording go to www.pcplanets.com/videoyoutube-Disney-intro.wSoUm8CK4RU.shtml.

2. Steve Martin, *Born Standing Up: A Comic's Life* (New York: Scribner, 2007).

3. Ibid. pp. 171–172.

4. Ibid. p. 197

5. CE represents Common Era, equivalent in a calendar to AD, which stands for *Anno Domini*—"In the year of our Lord."

6. The first nation to give Jews the right to vote was the United States of America. The European countries followed America in recognizing Jews as citizens with the right to hold public office and to vote. See Arthur Hertzberg, *The Jews in America* (New York: Simon and Schuster, 1989), pp. 72–73.

7. Rodger Kamenetz, *The Jew in the Lotus: A Poet's Rediscovery of Jewish Identity in Buddhist India* (New York: HarperOne, 1995), p. 3.

8. My sister Livia is named for my father's sister and my sister Helene for my mother's mother.

9. Words of Heddy Spitz: "After six months in Auschwitz, my three sisters and I found our bodies were filthy and we were

skeletons, weighing seventy or eighty pounds, surviving on one cup of soup made of bitter leaves each day. One cold morning we stood silently for two hours in line, waiting to have numbers put on our arms. Suddenly the line stopped. It was truly a miracle, because if we had had a number we would never have escaped. Without the number, we were later able to pass as Russian girls. I prayed to God to give me the strength to carry on.

"In the winter of 1944 the Gestapo ordered all of us who they had picked onto a train. After three days and three nights we were marched 120 kilometers through the snow, many without shoes, and ordered to dig. We sisters looked at each other. Was this the end? Finally the soldiers ordered us to stop and took us to a barn. Every day we were on the front digging trenches for tanks. My hands and feet were frozen, no covers, no water, no food. But I wanted to live.

"It was before Christmas. Suddenly, a German commander appeared and shouted, 'All out!' The Russians were coming. We had to march back to Germany. I was really weak. My feet were frozen so that they could hardly move. We marched for six weeks, from morning to night. I told my sisters that I could not go on. But they refused to leave me. 'If you are going to die, we will die together,' they agreed.

"That night we slept in a barn with a lot of straw. When the German soldiers ordered everyone out of the barn in the morning, we remained hidden under the straw. They brought in German shepherds that sniffed out eleven girls. Gunshots rang out, screams, silence. We heard the transport march on without us. Then the farmer came into the barn and announced, 'Five of you are perhaps still here. Tonight a troop of German soldiers will be staying in this barn. I feel sorry for you. I will leave some food. But you need to leave!'

"We waited for a long time. Then we got up and quickly ran out the back gate. We ran into the woods and did not look back. We started walking with renewed hope."

10. *Marah shekhorah*, Hebrew for bitter darkness, also meant black bile, like the Greek word *melancholia*. For as the Talmud states, irritable, aggressive behavior was considered a result of an excess of bile (see *Ketubot* 103b; *Bava Metzia* 107b).

11. The Bible is rich in stories of despair. Although in this book we focus on the lives of Moses, Rachel, and Job, there are many other examples, among them the following:

- Naomi, whose husband and two sons die while they are living in Moab. Upon returning to Israel she tells the locals who greet her, "Call me *Marah* (embittered one), for the Almighty has made my lot very bitter" (Ruth 1:20).

- Jonah, the prophet whom God asks to preach repentance to Israel's enemy, flees, taking a boat to Tarshish, a trip marked by stormy seas. Jonah sleeps through the turbulence until awakened by the sailors. Jonah says to them, "Toss me overboard and the sea will calm down for you; for I know that this terrible storm came upon you on my account" (Jonah 1:11), and reluctantly they comply. Later the prophet fulfills God's demand, the people of Nineveh repent, and they are forgiven; the depressed prophet prays, "Please, Lord, take my life, for I would rather die than live" (Jonah 4:3).

- Elijah the prophet, pursued by Queen Jezebel after he had slain idolatrous prophets, flees to the desert. "He came to a broom bush and sat down under it, and prayed that he might die. 'Now, O Lord, take my life, for I am no better than my fathers'" (I Kings 19:4).

12. As is the nature of Hebrew, there are a variety of possible translations. The Hebrew of Genesis 30:1 is often translated "If not, I am dead." Alternatively, "If not, let me die" is chosen by Rabbi Aryeh Kaplan in his work *The Living Torah* (New York: Maznaim Publishing, 1981), p. 139.

13. Ethical wills are grounded in the biblical tradition of blessing the next generation with a statement of hopes and values— such as Isaac blessing his sons (Gen. 27–28); Jacob blessing his grandsons and sons (Gen. 48–49); and Moses blessing the people (Deut. 33). The writing of ethical wills flourished in the Middle Ages—see the collection contained in Israel Abrahams, ed., *Hebrew Ethical Wills*, 2 vols. (Philadelphia: Jewish Publication Society, 1926). For a survey of Jewish ethical wills, with an emphasis on the modern era and a guide on composing your own, see Jack Riemer and Nathaniel Stampfer, *So That Your Values Live On: Ethical Wills and How to Prepare Them* (Woodstock, VT: Jewish Lights Publishing, 1991).

Chapter One

1. Born in Jerusalem, Isaac Luria was raised after his father's death in the home of his uncle in Egypt, who would later become his father-in-law. He moved to Safed, Israel, in his mid-thirties to study with the premier Kabbalist of his day, Moses Cordevero. After his master's death, Luria began to teach his original system of theoretical Kabbalah and to guide his select disciples into the practical Kabbalah of communing with the souls of the righteous. He taught for only two years, before he died in an epidemic. His teaching grew in influence through the writing of his disciples, primarily Hayyim Vital, who would dedicate the next twenty years of his life to recording what he had learned from Luria. For more on the life of Luria, read Lawrence Fine, *Physician of the Soul, Healer of the Cosmos: Isaac Luria and His Kabbalistic Fellowship* (Stanford, CA: Stanford University Press, 2003).

2. For further inquiry on the parallels between the big bang theory of contemporary physics and Luria's description of creation, see Daniel C. Matt, *God and the Big Bang: Discovering Harmony Between Science and Spirituality* (Woodstock, VT: Jewish Lights Publishing, 1998) and Richard Elliott Friedman, *The Disappearance of God: A Divine Mystery* (New York: Little, Brown, 1995).

3. A midrash states "And Jacob's anger was kindled": "Said the Holy One blessed be He to him, 'Is this the way to answer the troubled? By your life, your sons are destined to stand before her (i.e., Joseph)'"—*Genesis Rabbah* 71:10.

4. Elie Wiesel, *Souls on Fire* (New York: Summit Books, 1972), p. 132.

5. Job proclaims, "I will speak in the anguish [*tzar*] of my spirit" (Job 7:11); also see the use of *tzar* in Job 6:23; 15:24; 16:9; 36:16, 19; 38:23; 41:7.

6. These words are an epitaph on Maimonides' tomb in Tiberias, Israel.

7. Abraham Joshua Heschel, *Maimonides: A Biography* (New York: Farrar, Straus and Giroux, 1982), p. 38.

8. Ibid. p. 74.

9. There are two Talmuds, collections of the discussions of the Rabbis about the meaning of the Mishnah: the Jerusalem

Talmud, edited in the fifth century CE, and the Babylonian
Talmud of the sixth century CE.

10. Heschel, p. 127

11. Ibid. p. 130.

12. Ibid. p. 18.

13. Arthur Green, *Tormented Master: The Life and Spiritual Quest of Rabbi Nahman of Bratslav* (Woodstock, VT: Jewish Lights Publishing, 2004), p. 27.

14. Ibid. p. 10.

15. Arthur Green is currently the Irving Brudnick Professor of Jewish Theology and Mysticism at Hebrew College in Newton Centre, Massachusetts, and rector of that institution's rabbinical school.

16. Ibid. p. 40.

17. Ibid. p. 71.

18. Ibid. p. 72.

19. Ibid. p. 86.

20. Wiesel, p. 177.

21. Green, p. 15.

22. Wiesel, p. 201.

23. There are other eighteenth and nineteenth century Hasidic masters, such as the Seer of Lublin (Rabbi Jacob Isaac Horowitz), Rabbi Elimelech of Lyzhansk, and Rabbi Menachem Mendel of Kotzk, who suffered from bouts of severe depression. See Zvi Mark, "Madness, Melancholy and Suicide in Early Hasidism," *Kabbalah: Journal for the Study of Jewish Mystical Texts* 12 (2004), pp. 27–44. See also, Elie Wiesel, *Four Hasidic Masters: and Their Struggle Against Melancholy* (Notre Dame: University of Notre Dame Press, 1978)

24. The four levels are identified as the literal, the allegorical, the homiletic, and the secret or mystical. See Benjamin Edidin Scolnic, "Traditional Methods of Bible Story," in *Etz Hayim: Torah and Commentary*, David Lieber, sr. ed. (New York: Rabbinical Assembly, United Synagogue of Conservative Judaism, 2000), pp. 1494–99; also see Ibn Ezra and Rashi at start of *Shir HaShirim*.

25. In the words of the second-century Israel sage Ben Bag Bag, "Turn it [Torah] over, turn it over, for all is in it" (*Pirkei Avot* 5:24).

26. Zalman M. Schachter-Shalomi, *Gate to the Heart: An Evolving Process* (Philadelphia: Aleph, 1993), see chart in the book's appendix. The fours worlds of creation are referred to by the mystics as *assiyah*, *yetzirah*, *beriah*, and *atzilut*.

27. Rabbi Schachter-Shalomi conveyed his four worlds counseling approach to me in private conversation.

28. Elie Kaplan Spitz, *Does the Soul Survive? A Jewish Journey to Belief in Afterlife, Past Lives and Living with Purpose* (Woodstock, VT: Jewish Lights Publishing, 2001).

29. Heschel, p. 26.

30. Quoted by Haim Handwerker in "Happy Hour: A Psychology Class at Harvard Is Not Just Academic," *World Jewish Digest*, July 2006, p. 9, translated from a Hebrew article in the newspaper *Haaretz*.

31. This telling is my own based on a popular Jewish folk story. A similar principle is contained in the following story of the Buddha: "A woman, overwhelmed by the death of her son, came to the Buddha and begged him to restore the boy to life. The Buddha told her that in order to do so, he needed a handful of earth from a house that had never experienced any death. Having visited every house in the village and come to see that none had escaped bereavement, the woman returned to the Buddha, who comforted her with words of love and wisdom." Told by Mattieu Ricard, *Happiness: A Guide to Developing Life's Most Important Skill* (New York: Little, Brown, 2006), p. 67.

32. One in four Americans suffer from major depression, referred to medically as "clinical depression," at some point in life (George Howe Colt, *The Enigma of Suicide* [New York: Scribner, 1991], p. 43). It affects more than 100 million people a year and is the world's leading cause of disability (Joshua Wolf Shenk, *Lincoln's Melancholy: How Depression Challenged a President and Fueled His Greatness* [New York: Houghton Mifflin, 2005], p. 8). It costs more in treatment and lost productivity than anything but heart disease (Andrew Solomon, "Our Great Depression," *New York Times* op-ed, November 17, 2006, A31). A considerably smaller ratio is offered by Eric R. Kandel, who writes that "depression affects about 5 percent of the world's population at some time in their lives" (*In Search of Memory* [New York: Norton, 2006], p. 359).

33. People may also choose to die for a higher cause. This is true of soldiers going to war and, as in some cases, jumping on a hand grenade to save their comrades. The formula for becoming a suicide bomber is the belief that you are a soldier fighting an enemy on behalf of God, coupled with the faith that dying (and killing) now offers the reward of a better life in the next world. In contrast, this book focuses on those who take their lives due to despair, an act grounded in psychological hopelessness. Many do so despite the awareness that it is condemned religiously.

34. William Styron, *Darkness Visible: A Memoir of Madness* (New York: Vintage, 1992), p. 7.

35. "In 2000, about a million people worldwide killed themselves—about equal to the number of deaths from war and homicide that year put together." Shenk, p. 8, citing among others, Gregg Easterbrook, *The Progress Paradox: How Life Gets Better While People Feel Worse* (New York: Random House, 2003), pp. 163–166. "Between one and two percent of all Americans die by suicide, and some four or five percent make a suicide attempt at some point in their lives." Colt, p. 10.

36. Among the famous who have taken their own lives are writers Ernest Hemingway, Jack London, Sylvia Plath, Spalding Gray, and Primo Levi; musicians Phil Ochs, Kurt Cobain, and Sid Vicious; artists Diane Arbus and Vincent van Gogh.

37. Other psalms to consider reading that relate to despair and overcoming it are: 6, 13, 16, 18, 22–23, 25, 27, 30–32, 34, 37–38, 42–43, 46, 51, 55–56, 59, 62–63, 69, 71, 73, 77, 84, 86, 88, 90–91, 94–95, 103, 107, 110, 116, 118–119, 121, 123–124, 130–131, 137–139, 141–143, 146–147, 150.

38. The one-hundredth episode of the television series *Touched by an Angel*, entitled "Psalm 151," describes a psalm a mother writes for her dying son. The psalm is sung on the show and is later entitled "Testify to Love."

Chapter Two

1. Gauguin's attempt to take his life failed and he lived for five more years before dying of syphilis.

2. Abraham Twerski, *Addictive Thinking: Understanding Self-Deception* (Center City, MN: Hazelden, 1997), p. 10.

3. Jane E. Brody, "Shock Therapy Loses Some of Its Shock Value," *New York Times*, September 19, 2006, p. D7; www.nytimes.com/ 2006/09/19/health/psychology/19brody.html?ref=health.

4. Meditation is a useful tool for dealing with depression, specifically by developing the awareness that we are not our thoughts, and for examining our thoughts in an arm's-length fashion. See Stephen C. Hayes with Spencer Smith, *Get Out of Your Mind and Into Your Life: The New Acceptance and Commitment Therapy* (Oakland, CA: New Harbinger Publications, 2005).

Chapter Three

1. The account is different in II Samuel 1:5–10, where the Amalekite messenger to King David, reporting on King Saul's defeat and death, reports that after falling on his sword, King Saul was still alive, pleaded that he be released from agony, and so the Amalekite slayed him.

2. The text at II Samuel 17:23 says that Ahitophel was "buried in the sepulcher of his father," meaning that he was not ostracized.

3. BCE denotes "before the Common Era," i.e. before the year 0.

4. The same verse is also anonymously explicated in *Genesis Rabbah* 34:13, probably from around the same time as Rabbi Elazar: "This includes one who strangles himself. You might think that even one with the plight of Saul is meant, therefore we have [the Hebrew word] *akh*. You might think, even one like Hananiah, Mishael and Azariah; therefore we have *akh* [which may mean 'however']." There is also a Talmudic citation that a person is shunned after taking his own life: "No law may be quoted in the name of one who surrenders himself to meet death for the words of the Torah" (*Bava Kamma* 61b). The premise that life is not ours to take will later be identified with the statement of Rabbi Elazar HaKappar (*Pirkei Avot* 4:29): "It is not your will that formed you, nor was it your will that gave you birth; it is not your will that makes you live, and it is not your will that brings you death."

5. Talmudic stories of suicide: *Roman soldiers who are promised the world to come because of the noble context of their suicide: Ta'anit* 19a—An officer charged with capturing Rabban Gamliel mounted the roof and flung himself down in order to receive a place in the world to come; *Avodah Zarah* 18a—The execu-

tioner of Rabbi Chanina ben Teradyon removed the moist wool from over the sage's heart, easing his passing, and then the Roman soldier jumped into the flame himself. *To avoid shame*: *Berakhot* 23a—A student left his tefillin in a hole by the side of a road before entering a privy. A passing prostitute picked up the tefillin, produced them in the house of study, saying, "So-and-so paid me with these." When the student learned of the event, he jumped off a roof; *Hullin* 94a—A man received a gift of a wine barrel he believed to be filled with oil. After guests arrived to enjoy the bounty of oil, the host learned that there was only oil floating on top of the wine and he hanged himself. *Gittin* 57b—Young captives on a boat believed that the Romans would abuse them for prostitution or the violent circus, and jumped overboard. *To honor God's name*: *Gittin* 57b—As the Syrian-Greeks took away a woman's seventh son for execution, she exclaimed, "My son, go and say to our father, Abraham, 'You bound one, but I have bound seven altars.'" She went up on the roof and jumped to her death. A voice from heaven proclaimed, "A joyful mother of children" (story similar to a story recorded in II Maccabees). In addition to the Talmudic sources, there are even *earlier layers of Jewish writings* that present suicide neutrally. Some examples: II Maccabees (written in Greek, second century BCE) 14:41–46, Ragesh, the most respected man in Judea, committed suicide to avoid arrest by Nicanor, agent of King Demetrius; 10:12, Ptolemy, accused of being a traitor for supporting the Jews in the Syrian-Greek court, poisoned himself. There are also *stories of mass suicide* during Roman occupation: Judean fighters in 69 CE threw themselves over the walls of Jotapata Fortress or on their swords (H. Graetz, *History of the Jews* [Philadelphia: Jewish Publication Society, 1956], pp. 276–290; in Masada 70 CE, Jews chose mass suicide over capture (Josephus, *War of the Jews*, 7:9). These mass communal suicides would also occur in Europe of the Middle Ages, such as five hundred in 1190 in York, England. Such acts would be justified by medieval rabbis as sanctification of God's name.

6. See *Smakhot*, chapter 2.
7. The Rabbis condemn suicide as an act, but after a death presume a lack of intent. See Benjamin Gesundheit, "Suicide—A

Halakhic and Moral Analysis of *Masekhet Semanhot*," chapter 2, Laws 1–6, *Tradition* 35:3–20 (2001).

8. A. J. Droge, "Suicide," *The Anchor Bible Dictionary*, vol. 6 (New York: Doubleday, 1992), p. 225.

9. R. Burton, *The Anatomy of Melancholy* (New York: Da Capo Press Book Co., 1971).

10. Mark Williams, *Cry of Pain*, found in Kay Redfield Jamison, *Night Falls Fast: Understanding Suicide* (New York: Vintage, 1999), p. 17.

11. Jamison, p. 18.

12. Maimonides, Mishneh Torah, *Hilkhot Rotzeakh* 11:5. The topic of self-injury is inconclusively debated at B. T. *Bava Kamma* 91b.

13. See Maimonides, *Hilkhot Avel* 1:11, and Karo, *Arukh Ha Shulkhan, Yoreh Deah* 345:1.

14. Rabbi Jacob ben Asher (the *Tur*) says that tearing the garments is only prohibited by distant relatives, but the immediate family is permitted (*Tur, Yoreh Deah* 345).

15. *Arukh Ha Shulkhan* 345:5. This rabbinic conclusion was taken one step further when in 2004, leaders of Judaism's Conservative movement ruled that a suicide is "to be treated like any other death, with the right of burial in a cemetery and the same rituals of mourning." The *teshuvah* was composed by Rabbi Kassel Abelson and approved by the Rabbinical Assembly Committee on Law and Standards in September 2005. A dramatic example of an Orthodox ruling on interment despite suicide is the ruling of the Sephardic chief rabbi of Israel, Shlomo Amar, who permitted the interment of Zionist founder Theodor Herzl's children, Pauline and Hans, alongside their father in Jerusalem on September 20, 2006. Seventy-six years earlier, Pauline, who had suffered from morphine addiction leading to multiple hospitalizations, took her life in Bordeaux, France, with a tranquilizer overdose. The next day, Hans killed himself. Rabbi Amar ruled that mental instability and the psychological stress upon learning of his sister's death allowed each of them to be buried in the national Jewish cemetery.

16. Harold S. Kushner, *When Bad Things Happen to Good People* (New York: Avon, 1981, 1983).

17. Amos Oz, *A Tale of Love and Darkness* (New York: Harvest Books, 2005), pp. 211, 212, 214.

18. When honoring a loved one lost to suicide or any form of death, the traditional prayer of memorial is the Kaddish. This prayer, found in every Jewish prayer book, is not a petition but a statement of faith. Curiously, the Kaddish does not mention death. Rather the prayer focuses on God's sovereignty and hope for a redeemed world. In the moment of grieving when the world appears chaotic, we acknowledge that there is a sovereign and more, that there is reason to be hopeful that there will yet come a day in which the world is made whole by God. Like Job and the psalmist, we acknowledge as mourners that we can never understand God's works or thoughts. In ancient times, the words of prayer were recited by scholars at the conclusion of each session of sacred text study. Nearly a thousand years later, the rabbinic sages chose the Kaddish prayer to be recited by mourners during the mourning period. Since the Kaddish became the prayer recited at the end of a life instead of at the end of a Torah study session, it reminds us that each life story is worthy of study for the lessons it contains and the sacred deeds it describes to us.

    Another notable fact about the Kaddish prayer is that its recitation requires the presence of a minyan, a quorum of ten Jewish adults. Hence, honoring a loved one's memory with this prayer draws a mourner into community. We know that despair feels like darkness, chaos, and aloneness. We proclaim aloud, in the presence of others, that God is sovereign. We assert that the world, despite brokenness, is filled with good and purpose. When our own loss feels unique—and that is the nature of suffering—the Kaddish brings us back into the congregation and connects us to our ancient tradition and to the generations before us.

19. When the renowned psychiatrist Dr. Elisabeth Kübler-Ross in 1969 wrote of the five stages of grieving, she included a stage that she called depression (*On Death and Dying* [New York: Scribner, 1969; 1997]). She defined the five stages as: denial and isolation, anger, bargaining, depression, and acceptance. For the mourner, the depression stage is marked by emotional pain and withdrawal from the day-to-day workings of the

world. Freud made the distinction between mourning and *melancholia*, the term he used to refer to what is now called *clinical depression*. Freud noted that to an outsider the two states might look similar but that there is a key difference: a person who is suffering from clinical depression will engage in self-hatred, feeling at her core that she is of no value, of no worth, just plain no good. See Sigmund Freud's *On Murder, Mourning and Melancholia*, Penguin Modern Classics Translated Texts, trans. by Michael Hulse (2005) pp. 201–18.

Chapter Four

1. The insecurity of those former slaves who departed from Egypt is reflected in the words of the ten spies, reporting to Moses and the Israelites after visiting the inhabitants of the Promised Land: "We felt like tiny grasshoppers. That's all we were to them in their eyes" (Num. 13:33).
2. See *M. T. Arakhin* 1:4; Rashi to Exodus 1:16. Also used in scripture as the opening of the womb just before a newborn's emergence; see II Kings 19:3, Isaiah 37:3, Hosea 13:13.
3. Other ancient cultures recognized the crisis-birth connection. In Hinduism, the figure of Ganeshah, represented as the god with the elephant head, is known as the lord of obstacles and beginnings.
4. Daniel Matt, *The Essential Kabbalah* (New York: HarperCollins, 1995), p. 15.
5. Bentley, G. E. *The Stranger from Paradise: A Biography of William Blake* (Paul Mellon Centre for Studies in British Art), (New Haven: Yale University Press, 2003). Learned from Rabbi David Wolpe at a public lecture in 2006.
6. William Blake (1757–1827), identified by some as a "glorious luminary," illustrated many works including the Book of Job. Throughout his life he was drawn to the Bible and believed that he both saw angels and actively communicated with his deceased brother, Robert. Wordsworth said of him, "There was no doubt that this poor man was mad, but there is something in the madness of this man which interests me more than the sanity of Lord Byron and Walter Scott." Although he lacked recognition or success in his own life, his influence grew profoundly after his death, most remarkably in the 1960s.

Among the contemporary singers who have adapted his poems to music are U2, Van Morrison, and Kathleen Yearwood; also an influence on poets Bob Dylan and Allen Ginsburg.

7. Abraham Joshua Heschel, *Maimonides: A Biography* (New York: Farrar, Straus and Giroux, 1982, originally 1935).

8. See Rambam's introduction to his Mishnah commentary.

9. Maimonides, *Guide for the Perplexed* 3:12, 3:10. Heschel also noted a change in Maimonides' humility (see *Maimonides*, p. 137) after the crisis, such as his comment in a letter, "Know that I have set myself the goal of behaving humbly in every action, even though it damages me in the eyes of the crowd," and his remark, "One should train oneself not to lose one's temper, about a thing at which one could rightfully get angry, one should not even get upset over things that normally justify annoyance." Maimonides' words reveal that he was striving for a humility that overcomes resentment and bitterness.

10. The First Temple in Jerusalem was destroyed by the Babylonians in 586 BCE.

11. Rebbe Nachman of Breslov used two terms for depression— *marah shekhorah* and *atzvut. Marah shekhorah*, identified with black bile, was linked with physical causes. Nachman said that the primary cause of *atzvut* was an inability to accept God's ways of dealing with that person. See Avraham Greenbaum, *The Wings of the Sun: Traditional Jewish Healing in Theory and Practice* (Jerusalem/New York: Breslov Research Institute, 1995), pp. 154–159. Rebbe Nachman identified negative emotions as the source of most illness. He went further, according to my friend Hana Matt, by identifying *atzvut* with idolatry, based on a word play in Psalm 115:4.

12. Edited excerpt from *Likutei Moharan* I, 282.

13. Ibid.

14. B. T. *Avodah Zarah* 54b.

15. Marla Cilley, known as Flylady, teaches through her website www.flylady.net the importance of baby steps. For instance, she addresses CHAOS—Can't Have Anyone Over Syndrome— and how getting organized is done one step at a time. Her approach, as witnessed by the posted testimonials, has helped many regain mental well-being.

16. A. Pletscher (1991), "The Discovery of Antidepressants: A Winding Path," *Journal of Cellular and Molecular Sciences*, volume 47 (1); see http://en.wikipedia.org/wiki/Antidepressant.

17. One course of treatment for depression is the use of medicines known as SSRIs (selective serotonin reuptake inhibitors). The theory is that depression occurs when the receiving cell is not sufficiently stimulated by naturally occurring chemicals and therefore cannot function normally. SSRIs inhibit the reuptake of the neurotransmitter serotonin into the sending cell so that the serotonin stays in the synapse longer and remains available to stimulate the receptor of the receiving cell. When the chemicals provided by antidepressant medicines do not prove effective in treating depression, another available option is ECT, which is usually used only after other medications have failed due to the possibility of serious side effects.

18. See Eric Steel's film documentary, "The Bridge of Death" (2006) dist. as of 2007 by Koch Lorber Films.

19. Christopher D'Olier Reeve (1952–2004). See Christopher Reeve, *Still Me* (NY: Random House, 1998) and http://en. wikipedia.org/wiki/Christopher_reeves.

20. For information on Candace Lightner see: www.activistcash. com/biography.cfm/bid/3508; www.dui.com/dui-library/victims/ personal-tragedy; http://en.wikipedia.org/wiki/Candy_ Lightner.

21. Sherri Mandell, *Blessing of a Broken Heart* (New Milford, CT: Toby Press, 2nd ed., 2003).

Chapter Five

1. Rashi (France, 1040–1105), the classic biblical commentator, presents two interpretations for "you shall be a blessing": Until now blessings were in my power, but I now entrust them to you and you shall bless whomever you wish; and when the first blessing is recited in the thrice-daily Amidah prayer, it will conclude with only your name, Abraham, rather than the other patriarchs as well.

2. *Pesikta de-Rab Kahana* 29, editor Salomon Buber (Lyck: Mekize Nedarim, 1868), 189a-b; *Pesikta de-Rab Kahana: R. Kahana's Compilation of Discourses for Sabbaths and Festal Days*, translated by William G. Braude and Israel J. Kapstein (Philadelphia: Jewish Publication Society, 1975), Piska 26, pp. 398–99.

3. Joshua Wolf Shenk, *Lincoln's Melancholy: How Depression Challenged a President and Fueled His Greatness* (New York: Houghton Mifflin, 2005).

4. Ibid. pp. 3–4, citing Milton H. Shutes, *Lincoln and the Doctors: A Medical Narrative of the Life of Abraham Lincoln* (New York: Pioneer Press, 1933), p. 74.

5. Even a few years later, a poem entitled "The Suicide's Soliloquy," published anonymously in the *Illinois Sangano Journal*, appears, according to Shenk, to have been submitted by the future president. The poem's final stanza reads: "Yes! I've resolved the deed to do / And this is the place to do it. / This heart I'll rush a dagger through / Though I in hell shall rue it!" Ibid., p. 40.

6. Ibid. p. 65.

7. Ibid. p. 197, citing B. B. Lloyd's interview with William Henry Herndon, November 29, 1866, *Herndon's Informants*, p. 426.

8. Shenk, p. 208, citing Johnson Brigham, *James Harlan* (Iowa City: State Historical Society of Iowa, 1913), p. 338.

9. Shenk, p. 207.

10. Winston Churchill's parents neglected him during his childhood. In letters from his boarding school, the Harrow School, he begs his mother, Lady Randolph, to either visit him or allow him to come home for visits. He would later say that he was hardly on speaking terms with his father. Instead, he developed a very close relationship with his nanny, whom he called "Woomany." See Roy Jenkins, *Churchill: A Biography* (New York: Farrar, Straus and Giroux, 2001), pp. 8–10; Wikipedia, http://en.wikipedia.org/wiki/Winston_Churchill. For an examination of how Churchill's depression enabled his greatness, consider Anthony Storr, *Churchill's Black Dog, Kafka's Mice and Other Phenomena of the Human Mind* (New York: HarperCollins, 1989, 1997), who wrote: "Had he been a stable and equable man, he could never have inspired the nation. In 1940, when all the odds were against Britain, a leader of sober judgment might well have concluded that we were finished."

11. Said by Max Aitken, later Lord Beaverbrook, cited in William Manchester's *The Bold Lion: Winston Spencer Churchill: Visions of Glory, 1874–1932* (Boston: Little, Brown, 1983), p. 24.

12. Manchester, p. 23.

13. Ibid. p. 25.

14. Another political and spiritual leader worthy of mention regarding the challenge of personal despair is Martin Luther King Jr. In 1967 he had taken an unpopular stand against the war in Vietnam. The civil rights movement with its marches and boycotts, had been met with much violence, including many threats on his life. The movement often felt stalled. Coretta Scott King, months before her husband's assassination, "would remember that he seemed caught, sluggish, passive, in the thrall of a depression 'greater than I had ever seen before.' To her worried queries, he would mutter, 'People expect me to have answers and I don't have any answers.' He was smoking more heavily, heedlessly.... 'I am tired of demonstrating,' he blurted openly more than once, 'I am tired of the threat of death. I want to live'" (Marshall Frady, *Martin Luther King Jr.: A Life* [New York: Penguin Books, 2002], p.189). Despite his private despair, he addressed a crowd from his higher self, saying the day before his murder: "because I've been to the mountaintop. And I don't mind. Like anybody, I would like to live a long time, longevity has its place. But I'm not concerned about that now, I just want to do God's will— And He's allowed me to go up to the mountain, and I've looked over, and I've seen the Promised Land! I may not get there with you. But I want you to know tonight that we, as a people, will get to the Promised Land! And so I'm happy tonight. I'm not fearing any man. Mine eyes have seen the glory of the coming of the Lord!" (Frady, pp. 202–203).

15. Martin Buber, *I and Thou*, translated by Walter Kaufman (New York: Scribners, 1970).

16. Martin Buber, *Between Man and Man* (New York: Macmillan, 1970; originally 1947), pp. 13–14.

17. "Investigators have repeatedly tried to single out specific 'therapeutic factors' that can distinguish good therapy from bad, and the only unequivocal winner is what's termed a 'positive therapeutic alliance,' meaning that the client feels that the therapist exhibits qualities like empathy and support." Laurie Abraham, "Can This Marriage Be Saved? A Year in the Life of Couples-Therapy Group," *New York Times Magazine*, August 12, 2007, p. 33.

18. B. T. *Nedarim* 39b: Rabbi Abba son of Rabbi Hanina said: He who visits an invalid takes away a sixtieth of his pain [or in another version a sixtieth of his illness]. A related story that conveys the need for outside intervention to affect a cure is the story of Rabbi Yohanan. He was a healer who had affected a cure by literally raising the hand of an ill friend. When Rabbi Yohanan became ill, another friend came to visit him, raised Rabbi Yohanan's hand, and freed him from his illness. The Talmud asks, "Why could Rabbi Yohanan [not] raise himself?" And answers, "It is said, 'The prisoner cannot free himself from prison'" (B. T. *Berakhot* 5b). It is as if to open a door, the key must be inserted from the outside.

19. Viktor Frankl, *Man's Search for Meaning* (New York: Washington Square Press, 1985; orig. 1946).

20. Gratitude to Professor Reuven Kimmelman for sharing this story with me, as shared with him by one of the participants. More on that initial visit with the Dalai Lama is found in Rodger Kamenetz, *The Jew in the Lotus: A Poet's Rediscovery of Jewish Identity in Buddhist India* (San Francisco: HarperSanFrancisco, 1994).

21. I quote Rabbi Hartman as I remember his words from class at Hebrew University of Jerusalem, more than thirty years ago. A scholarly examination of God having a personality is found in Hartman's foreword to Yochanan Muffs's, *The Personhood of God: Biblical Theology, Human Faith and the Divine Image* (Woodstock, VT: Jewish Lights Publishing, 2005).

22. "Noah" reversed in the Hebrew spells *chen*, (grace).

23. Avivah Zornberg, *Genesis: The Beginning of Desire* (Philadelphia: Jewish Publication Society, 1995), p. 39.

24. At Sinai, following the revelation of the Ten Commandments, the Israelites affirm their commitment, saying, "Everything that the Ever-Present-One has said, we will do and we will listen" (Exod. 24:7).

25. The Bible states that the "whole nation ... stood under the mountain" (Exod. 19:17). Rashi, commenting on this verse, cites the Talmudic statement, "The Almighty held the mountain over them like a canopy," threatening them with death if they would not accept the commandments (B. T. *Shabbat* 88a). The Zohar accepts the interpretation that the mountain was

held over them like a canopy and uses it to represent a canopy of commitment, a nuptial canopy (a *huppah*) of love and marriage.

26. Writing in sixteenth-century Turkey and Israel, Rabbi Moses Alshekh comments on these verses: "Anger bottled up inside can lead to an explosion while acknowledging emotions and understanding pain leads to healing." *Itturei Torah* (Tel Aviv: Yavneh, 1985) (Hebrew) on Numbers 32:7–9. Implicit in God's words to Moses, "Do not try to stop me," is an invitation to challenge God's decision.

27. A midrash, an early rabbinic imagining, states that because God is subject to divine law too, God stood before a seated Moses serving as God's judge in order to release God from the vow of destruction. *Exodus Rabbah* 43:4; Louis Ginzberg, *Legends of the Jews*, vol. 1 (Philadelphia: Jewish Publication Society, 2003), p. 128, citing "unknown midrash in Yalkut Reubeni Num. 30:14."

28. M. T. *Hilkhot Teshuvah* ch. 2.

29. Yet, in this case there is a new element to Moses's plea. Moses reminds God of the words spoken at Mount Sinai, "The Ever-Present-One, slow to anger, abundant in kindness, forgiver of iniquity and willful sin ..." (Num. 14:18). Moses does not quote God precisely, but edits the list of qualities God had proclaimed, "compassionate and gracious," and omits the statement that God "abounds ... in truth."

30. See Rabbi Daniel Pressman's "Torah Sparks" for *Parshat Shelach Lecha*, 5754, United Synagogue of Conservative Judaism.

31. Maimonides, *Guide for the Perplexed* 3:32.

32. B. *Yevamot* 71a; B. T. *Baba Metzia* 31b; also see Maimonides, *Guide* 1:29–33; 65–66.

33. For classical sources that make the link between these words, see *Bereshit Rabbah*, Albeck edition [Hebrew], *parashah* 39; and Ramban's *HaEmunah v'Habitakhon*, *perek* 19.

34. *Sifrei, Deuteronomy, Ekev*. Also see B. T. *Sotah* 14a.

35. *The Big Book*, 4th ed. (New York: Alcoholics Anonymous World Services Publishing, 2004), p. 124.

Suggestions for Further Reading

The Blues and Major Depression

The Big Book, 4th ed. (New York: Alcoholics Anonymous World Services Publishing, 2004).The classic, practical guide to overcoming compulsive behavior.

David Burns, *Feeling Good: The New Mood Therapy* (New York: Avon, 1980, 1999). Using the tools of cognitive therapy, this book offers practical guidance on changing negative thoughts.

Arthur Green, *Tormented Master: The Life and Spiritual Quest of Rabbi Nahman of Bratslov* (Woodstock, VT: Jewish Lights, 2004). A biography of an important Jewish teacher who used his depression as a source of teaching and even greatness.

Rabbi Abraham Joshua Heschel, *Maimonides: A Biography* (New York: Farrar, Straus and Giroux, 1982). A paean to the monumental life of Maimonides, who was seared by depression, and yet was known for his stability and wisdom.

Ernest Kurtz and Katherine Ketcham, *The Spirituality of Imperfection: Storytelling and the Search for Meaning* (New York: Bantam Books, 1993). Collection of wisdom stories that offer acceptance of human frailty.

Eric Maisel, *The Van Gogh Blues: The Creative Person's Path through Depression* (New York: Rodale, 2002). Links increased risk of depression to artistic personalities and their quest for meaning.

Joshua Wolf Shenk, *Lincoln's Melancholy: How Depression Challenged a President and Fueled His Greatness* (New York: Houghton Mifflin, 2005). Portrays a great man struggling with depression and offers a learned description of the nature of depression.

Andrew Solomon, *The Noonday Demon: An Atlas of Depression* (New York: Scribner, 2001, 2003). Offers a comprehensive examination of depression.

William Styron, *Darkness Visible: A Memoir of Madness* (New York: Vintage, 1990). The author of *Sophie's Choice* masterfully describes his anguish in the tunnel of despair.

Abraham J. Twerski, *Addictive Thinking: Understanding Self-Deception* (Center City, MN: Hazelden, 1997). A psychiatrist with a specialty in addictions examines the nature of compulsive thought and deception.

Suicide

George Howe Colt, *The Enigma of Suicide: A Timely Investigation into the Causes, the Possibilities for Prevention and the Paths to Healing* (New York: Scriber, 1991). A comprehensive examination of the factors that lead to suicide and a history of society's reactions to suicide.

Carla Fine, *No Time to Say Goodbye: Surviving the Suicide of a Loved One* (New York: Broadway, 1997). Painful descriptions of processing loss, marked by insight and healing.

Eric Marcus, *Why Suicide?: Answers to 200 of the Most Frequently Asked Questions about Suicide, Attempted Suicide, and Assisted Suicide* (New York: HarperOne, 1996). Provides straightforward, informed answers.

Edwin S. Shneidman, *The Suicidal Mind* (New York: Oxford Press, 1996). The physician who coined the term and the field of *suicidology* describes the nature of the person at risk.

Related Jewish Books

Breslov Research Institute, *The Empty Chair: Finding Hope and Joy—Timeless Wisdom from a Hasidic Master, Rebbe Nachman of Breslov* (Woodstock, VT: Jewish Lights, 1994).

———, *The Gentle Weapon: Prayers for Everyday and Not-So-Everyday Moments—Timeless Wisdom from the Teachings of the Hasidic Master, Rebbe Nachman of Breslov* (Woodstock, VT: Jewish Lights, 1999).

Elliot N. Dorff, *Matters of Life and Death: A Jewish Approach to Modern Medical Ethics* (Philadelphia: Jewish Publication Society, 1998). Describes, among other topics, Jewish views on stewardship of the body and suicide.

Avraham Greenbaum, *The Wings of the Sun: Traditional Jewish Healing in Theory and Practice* (New York/Jerusalem: Breslov Research Institute, 1995). A guide to Jewish healing, with an emphasis on Hasidic insights, particularly those of Rebbe Nachman of Breslov.

Karyn D. Kedar, *The Bridge to Forgiveness: Stories and Prayers for Finding God and Restoring Wholeness* (Woodstock, VT: Jewish Lights, 2007).

Harold S. Kushner, *When Bad Things Happen to Good People* (New York: Avon, 1981, 1983). A rabbi's search in the shadow of tragedy to reclaim a relationship with God through a reinterpretation of the Book of Job.

Naomi Levy, *To Begin Again: The Journey toward Comfort, Strength, and Faith in Difficult Times* (New York: Ballantine, 1999). Jewish wrestling with, and wisdom from, tragedy.

Kerry M. Olitzky, *Jewish Paths toward Healing and Wholeness: A Personal Guide to Dealing with Suffering* (Woodstock, VT: Jewish Lights, 2000).

———, *Restful Reflections* (Woodstock, VT: Jewish Lights, 2001).

———, *Sacred Intentions* (Woodstock, VT: Jewish Lights, 1999).

Kerry M. Olitzky and Stuart Copans, *Twelve Jewish Steps to Recovery: A Personal Guide to Turning from Alcoholism and Other Addictions* (Woodstock, VT: Jewish Lights Publishing, 1991). Culls Jewish quotes and practical guidance on overcoming addictions.

Abraham J. Twerski, *Happiness and the Human Spirit: The Spirituality of Becoming the Best Person Your Can Be* (Woodstock, VT: Jewish Lights Publishing, 2007). Harvests a lifetime of spiritual study, psychological counseling, and life experience.

David J. Wolpe and Mitch Albom, *Making Loss Matter: Creating Meaning in Difficult Times* (New York: Riverhead, 2000). Uplifting, personally based guidance on making life matter in the face of loss.

AVAILABLE FROM BETTER BOOKSTORES.
TRY YOUR BOOKSTORE FIRST.

Bar/Bat Mitzvah

The JGirl's Guide: The Young Jewish Woman's Handbook for Coming of Age
By Penina Adelman, Ali Feldman, and Shulamit Reinharz
This inspirational, interactive guidebook helps pre-teen Jewish girls address the many issues surrounding coming of age.   6 x 9, 240 pp, Quality PB, 978-1-58023-215-9 **$14.99**

Also Available: **The JGirl's Teacher's and Parent's Guide**
8½ x 11, 56 pp, PB, 978-1-58023-225-8 **$8.99**

Bar/Bat Mitzvah Basics: A Practical Family Guide to Coming of Age Together
Edited by Cantor Helen Leneman   6 x 9, 240 pp, Quality PB, 978-1-58023-151-0 **$18.95**

The Bar/Bat Mitzvah Memory Book, 2nd Edition: An Album for Treasuring the Spiritual Celebration *By Rabbi Jeffrey K. Salkin and Nina Salkin*
8 x 10, 48 pp, Deluxe HC, 2-color text, ribbon marker, 978-1-58023-263-0 **$19.99**

For Kids—Putting God on Your Guest List, 2nd Edition: How to Claim the Spiritual Meaning of Your Bar or Bat Mitzvah *By Rabbi Jeffrey K. Salkin*
6 x 9, 144 pp, Quality PB, 978-1-58023-308-8 **$15.99** *For ages 11–13*

Putting God on the Guest List, 3rd Edition: How to Reclaim the Spiritual Meaning of Your Child's Bar or Bat Mitzvah *By Rabbi Jeffrey K. Salkin*
6 x 9, 224 pp, Quality PB, 978-1-58023-222-7 **$16.99**; HC, 978-1-58023-260-9 **$24.99**

Also Available: **Putting God on the Guest List Teacher's Guide**
8½ x 11, 48 pp, PB, 978-1-58023-226-5 **$8.99**

Tough Questions Jews Ask: A Young Adult's Guide to Building a Jewish Life
By Rabbi Edward Feinstein 6 x 9, 160 pp, Quality PB, 978-1-58023-139-8 **$14.99** *For ages 12 & up*

Also Available: **Tough Questions Jews Ask Teacher's Guide**
8½ x 11, 72 pp, PB, 978-1-58023-187-9 **$8.95**

Bible Study/Midrash

Abraham's Bind & Other Bible Tales of Trickery, Folly, Mercy and Love *By Michael J. Caduto*
Re-imagines many biblical characters, retelling their stories.
6 x 9, 224 pp, HC, 978-1-59473-186-0 **$19.99** *(A SkyLight Paths book)*

Ancient Secrets: Using the Stories of the Bible to Improve Our Everyday Lives
By Rabbi Levi Meier, PhD 5½ x 8½, 288 pp, Quality PB, 978-1-58023-064-3 **$16.95**

The Genesis of Leadership: What the Bible Teaches Us about Vision, Values and Leading Change *By Rabbi Nathan Laufer; Foreword by Senator Joseph I. Lieberman*
Unlike other books on leadership, this one is rooted in the stories of the Bible.
6 x 9, 288 pp, Quality PB, 978-1-58023-352-1 **$18.99**; HC, 978-1-58023-241-8 **$24.99**

Hineini in Our Lives: Learning How to Respond to Others through 14 Biblical Texts and Personal Stories *By Norman J. Cohen* 6 x 9, 240 pp, Quality PB, 978-1-58023-274-6 **$16.99**

Moses and the Journey to Leadership: Timeless Lessons of Effective Management from the Bible and Today's Leaders *By Dr. Norman J. Cohen*
6 x 9, 240 pp, Quality PB, 978-1-58023-351-4 **$18.99**; HC, 978-1-58023-227-2 **$21.99**

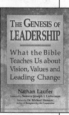

Self, Struggle & Change: Family Conflict Stories in Genesis and Their Healing Insights for Our Lives *By Norman J. Cohen* 6 x 9, 224 pp, Quality PB, 978-1-879045-66-8 **$18.99**

The Triumph of Eve & Other Subversive Bible Tales *By Matt Biers-Ariel*
5½ x 8½, 192 pp, Quality PB, 978-1-59473-176-1 **$14.99**; HC, 978-1-59473-040-5 **$19.99**
(A SkyLight Paths book)

The Wisdom of Judaism: An Introduction to the Values of the Talmud
By Rabbi Dov Peretz Elkins
Explores the essence of Judaism.   6 x 9, 192 pp, Quality PB, 978-1-58023-327-9 **$16.99**

Also Available: **The Wisdom of Judaism Teacher's Guide**
8½ x 11, 18 pp, PB, 978-1-58023-350-7 **$8.99**

Or phone, fax, mail or e-mail to: **JEWISH LIGHTS** Publishing
Sunset Farm Offices, Route 4 • P.O. Box 237 • Woodstock, Vermont 05091
Tel: (802) 457-4000 • Fax: (802) 457-4004 • www.jewishlights.com

Credit card orders: **(800) 962-4544** (8:30AM–5:30PM ET Monday–Friday)
Generous discounts on quantity orders. SATISFACTION GUARANTEED. Prices subject to change.

Categories/Topics continued:

Judaism / Living a Jewish Life

Bar and Bat Mitzvah's Meaning: Preparing Spiritually with Your Child

Choosing a Congregation That Is Right for You

Considering Judaism: Choosing a Faith, Joining a People

Do Jews Believe in the Soul's Survival?

Exploring Judaism as an Adult

Jewish Meditation: How to Begin Your Practice

There's a Place for Us: Gays and Lesbians in the Jewish Community

To Meet Your Soul Mate, You Must Meet Your Soul

Yearning for God

Family Issues

Jewish Adoption: Unique Issues, Practical Solutions

Are You Being Hurt by Someone You Love? Domestic Abuse in the Jewish Community

Grandparenting Interfaith Grandchildren

Healing Estrangement in Your Family Relationships

Interfaith Families Making Jewish Choices

Jewish Approaches to Parenting Teens

Looking Back on Divorce and Letting Go

Parenting through a Divorce

Raising a Child with Special Needs

Talking to Your Children about God

Spiritual Care / Personal Growth

Bringing Your Sadness to God

Doing Teshuvah: Undoing Mistakes, Repairing Relationships and Finding Inner Peace

Easing the Burden of Stress

Finding a Way to Forgive

Finding the Help You Need: Psychotherapy, Pastoral Counseling, and the Promise of Spiritual Direction

Praying in Hard Times: The Soul's Imaginings

Surviving a Crisis or a Tragedy

Now available in hundreds of congregations, health-care facilities, funeral homes, colleges and military installations, these helpful, comforting resources can be uniquely presented in *LifeLights* display racks, available from Jewish Lights. Each *LifeLight* topic is sold in packs of twelve for $9.95. General discounts are available for quantity purchases.

Visit us online at www.jewishlights.com for a complete list of titles, authors, prices and ordering information, or call us at (802) 457-4000 or toll free at (800) 962-4544.

Pastoral Care Resources
LifeLights/™אורות החיים

LifeLights/™אורות החיים are inspirational, information-al booklets about challenges to our emotional and spiritual lives and how to deal with them. Offering help for wholeness and healing, each *LifeLight* is written from a uniquely Jewish spiritual perspective by a wise and caring soul—someone who knows the inner territory of grief, doubt, confusion and longing.

In addition to providing wise words to light a diffi-cult path, each *LifeLight* booklet provides suggestions for additional resources for reading. Many list organi-zations, Jewish and secular, that can provide help, along with information on how to contact them.

> "Invaluable for those needing comfort and
> instruction in times of difficulty and loss."
> **Rabbi David Wolpe**, Sinai Temple, Los Angeles, CA

> "Particularly useful for hospital visits and shiva calls—and
> they enable me to help at those times when I feel helpless."
> **Rabbi Sally Priesand**, Monmouth Reform Temple,
> Tinton Falls, NJ

Categories/Topics:

Health & Healing

Abortion and Judaism: Rabbinic Opinion and Jewish Law
Caring for Your Aging Parents
Caring for Yourself/When Someone Is Ill
Facing and Recovering from Surgery
Facing Cancer as a Family
Finding Spiritual Strength in Pain or Illness
Jewish Response to Dementia: Honoring Broken Tablets
Living with Cancer, One Day at a Time
Recognizing a Loved One's Addiction, and Providing Help
**When Madness Comes Home: Living in the Shadow of a
    Loved One's Mental Illness**

Loss / Grief / Death & Dying

Coping with the Death of a Spouse
**From Death through Shiva: A Guide to Jewish Grieving
    Practices**
Jewish Hospice: To Live, to Hope, to Heal
Making Sacred Choices at the End of Life
Mourning a Miscarriage
Taking the Time You Need to Mourn Your Loss
Talking to Children about Death
When Someone You Love Is Dying
When Someone You Love Needs Long-Term Care

Children's Books
by Sandy Eisenberg Sasso

Adam & Eve's First Sunset: God's New Day
Engaging new story explores fear and hope, faith and gratitude in ways that will delight kids and adults—inspiring us to bless each of God's days and nights.
9 x 12, 32 pp, Full-color illus., HC, 978-1-58023-177-0 **$17.95** *For ages 4 & up*

Also Available as a Board Book: Adam and Eve's New Day
5 x 5, 24 pp, Full-color illus., Board, 978-1-59473-205-8 **$7.99** *For ages 0–4 (A SkyLight Paths book)*

But God Remembered
Stories of Women from Creation to the Promised Land
Four different stories of women—Lillith, Serach, Bityah, and the Daughters of Z—teach us important values through their faith and actions.
9 x 12, 32 pp, Full-color illus., Quality PB, 978-1-58023-372-9 **$8.99**; HC, 978-1-879045-43-9
$16.95 *For ages 8 & up*

Cain & Abel: Finding the Fruits of Peace
Shows children that we have the power to deal with anger in positive ways. Provides questions for kids and adults to explore together.
9 x 12, 32 pp, Full-color illus., HC, 978-1-58023-123-7 **$16.95** *For ages 5 & up*

God in Between
If you wanted to find God, where would you look? This magical, mythical tale teaches that God can be found where we are: within all of us and the relationships between us.
9 x 12, 32 pp, Full-color illus., HC, 978-1-879045-86-6 **$16.95** *For ages 4 & up*

God's Paintbrush: Special 10th Anniversary Edition
Wonderfully interactive, invites children of all faiths and backgrounds to encounter God through moments in their own lives. Provides questions adult and child can explore together.
11 x 8½, 32 pp, Full-color illus., HC, 978-1-58023-195-4 **$17.95** *For ages 4 & up*

Also Available: God's Paintbrush Teacher's Guide
8½ x 11, 32 pp, PB, 978-1-879045-57-6 **$8.95**

God's Paintbrush Celebration Kit
A Spiritual Activity Kit for Teachers and Students of All Faiths, All Backgrounds
Additional activity sheets available:
8-Student Activity Sheet Pack (40 sheets/5 sessions), 978-1-58023-058-2 **$19.95**
Single-Student Activity Sheet Pack (5 sessions), 978-1-58023-059-9 **$3.95**

In God's Name
Like an ancient myth in its poetic text and vibrant illustrations, this award-winning modern fable about the search for God's name celebrates the diversity and, at the same time, the unity of all people.
9 x 12, 32 pp, Full-color illus., HC, 978-1-879045-26-2 **$16.99** *For ages 4 & up*

Also Available as a Board Book: What Is God's Name?
5 x 5, 24 pp, Board, Full-color illus., 978-1-893361-10-2 **$7.99** *For ages 0–4 (A SkyLight Paths book)*

Also Available: In God's Name video and study guide
Computer animation, original music, and children's voices. 18 min. **$29.99**

Also Available in Spanish: El nombre de Dios
9 x 12, 32 pp, Full-color illus., HC, 978-1-893361-63-8 **$16.95** *(A SkyLight Paths book)*

Noah's Wife: The Story of Naamah
When God tells Noah to bring the animals of the world onto the ark, God also calls on Naamah, Noah's wife, to save each plant on Earth. Based on an ancient text.
9 x 12, 32 pp, Full-color illus., HC, 978-1-58023-134-3 **$16.95** *For ages 4 & up*

Also Available as a Board Book: Naamah, Noah's Wife
5 x 5, 24 pp, Board, 978-1-893361-56-0 **$7.95** *For ages 0–4 (A SkyLight Paths book)*

For Heaven's Sake: Finding God in Unexpected Places
9 x 12, 32 pp, Full-color illus., HC, 978-1-58023-054-4 **$16.95** *For ages 4 & up*

God Said Amen: Finding the Answers to Our Prayers
9 x 12, 32 pp, Full-color illus., HC, 978-1-58023-080-3 **$16.95** *For ages 4 & up*

Current Events/History

A Dream of Zion: American Jews Reflect on Why Israel Matters to Them
Edited by Rabbi Jeffrey K. Salkin Explores what Jewish people in America have to say about Israel. 6 x 9, 304 pp, HC, 978-1-58023-340-8 **$24.99**
Also Available: **A Dream of Zion Teacher's Guide** 8½ x 11, 18 pp, PB, 978-1-58023-356-9 **$8.99**

The Jewish Connection to Israel, the Promised Land: A Brief Introduction for Christians *By Rabbi Eugene Korn, PhD* 5½ x 8½, 192 pp, Quality PB, 978-1-58023-318-7 **$14.99**

The Story of the Jews: A 4,000-Year Adventure—A Graphic History Book
Written & illustrated by Stan Mack 6 x 9, 288 pp, illus., Quality PB, 978-1-58023-155-8 **$16.99**

Hannah Senesh: Her Life and Diary, the First Complete Edition
By Hannah Senesh; Foreword by Marge Piercy; Preface by Eitan Senesh
6 x 9, 368 pp, Quality PB, 978-1-58023-342-2 **$19.99**; 352 pp, HC, 978-1-58023-212-8 **$24.99**

The Ethiopian Jews of Israel: Personal Stories of Life in the Promised Land *By Len Lyons, PhD; Foreword by Alan Dershowitz; Photographs by Ilan Ossendryver* Recounts, through photographs and words, stories of Ethiopian Jews.
10½ x 10, 240 pp, 100 full-color photos, HC, 978-1-58023-323-1 **$34.99**

Foundations of Sephardic Spirituality: The Inner Life of Jews of the Ottoman Empire
By Rabbi Marc D. Angel, PhD 6 x 9, 224 pp, HC, 978-1-58023-243-2 **$24.99**

Judaism and Justice: The Jewish Passion to Repair the World
By Rabbi Sidney Schwarz 6 x 9, 352 pp, Quality PB, 978-1-58023-353-8 **$19.99**

Ecology/Environment

A Wild Faith: Jewish Ways into Wilderness, Wilderness Ways into Judaism
By Rabbi Mike Comins; Foreword by Nigel Savage
Offers ways to enliven and deepen your spiritual life through wilderness experience.
6 x 9, 240 pp, Quality PB, 978-1-58023-316-3 **$16.99**

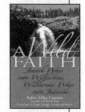

Ecology & the Jewish Spirit: Where Nature & the Sacred Meet
Edited by Ellen Bernstein 6 x 9, 288 pp, Quality PB, 978-1-58023-082-7 **$18.99**

Torah of the Earth: Exploring 4,000 Years of Ecology in Jewish Thought
Vol. 1: Biblical Israel: One Land, One People; Rabbinic Judaism: One People, Many Lands
Vol. 2: Zionism: One Land, Two Peoples; Eco-Judaism: One Earth, Many Peoples
Edited by Arthur Waskow Vol. 1: 6 x 9, 272 pp, Quality PB, 978-1-58023-086-5 **$19.95**
Vol. 2: 6 x 9, 336 pp, Quality PB, 978-1-58023-087-2 **$19.95**

The Way Into Judaism and the Environment
By Jeremy Benstein 6 x 9, 224 pp, HC, 978-1-58023-268-5 **$24.99**

Grief/Healing

Healing and the Jewish Imagination: Spiritual and Practical Perspectives on Judaism and Health *Edited by Rabbi William Cutter, PhD* Explores Judaism for comfort in times of illness and perspectives on suffering.
6 x 9, 240 pp, HC, 978-1-58023-314-9 **$24.99**

Grief in Our Seasons: A Mourner's Kaddish Companion *By Rabbi Kerry M. Olitzky*
4½ x 6¼, 448 pp, Quality PB, 978-1-879045-55-2 **$15.95**

Healing of Soul, Healing of Body: Spiritual Leaders Unfold the Strength & Solace in Psalms *Edited by Rabbi Simkha Y. Weintraub, CSW*
6 x 9, 128 pp, 2-color illus. text, Quality PB, 978-1-879045-31-6 **$14.99**

Mourning & Mitzvah, 2nd Edition: A Guided Journal for Walking the Mourner's Path through Grief to Healing *By Anne Brener, LCSW*
7½ x 9, 304 pp, Quality PB, 978-1-58023-113-8 **$19.99**

Tears of Sorrow, Seeds of Hope, 2nd Edition: A Jewish Spiritual Companion for Infertility and Pregnancy Loss *By Rabbi Nina Beth Cardin*
6 x 9, 208 pp, Quality PB, 978-1-58023-233-3 **$18.99**

A Time to Mourn, a Time to Comfort, 2nd Edition: A Guide to Jewish Bereavement *By Dr. Ron Wolfson*
7 x 9, 384 pp, Quality PB, 978-1-58023-253-1 **$19.99**

When a Grandparent Dies: A Kid's Own Remembering Workbook for Dealing with Shiva and the Year Beyond *By Nechama Liss-Levinson, PhD*
8 x 10, 48 pp, 2-color text, HC, 978-1-879045-44-6 **$15.95** *For ages 7–13*

Theology/Philosophy/The Way Into... Series

The Way Into... series offers an accessible and highly usable "guided tour" of the Jewish faith, people, history and beliefs—in total, an introduction to Judaism that will enable you to understand and interact with the sacred texts of the Jewish tradition. Each volume is written by a leading contemporary scholar and teacher, and explores one key aspect of Judaism. *The Way Into...* series enables all readers to achieve a real sense of Jewish cultural literacy through guided study.

The Way Into Encountering God in Judaism
By Neil Gillman
For everyone who wants to understand how Jews have encountered God throughout history and today.
6 x 9, 240 pp, Quality PB, 978-1-58023-199-2 **$18.99**; HC, 978-1-58023-025-4 **$21.95**
Also Available: **The Jewish Approach to God:** A Brief Introduction for Christians
By Neil Gillman
5½ x 8¼, 192 pp, Quality PB, 978-1-58023-190-9 **$16.95**

The Way Into Jewish Mystical Tradition
By Lawrence Kushner
Allows readers to interact directly with the sacred mystical text of the Jewish tradition. An accessible introduction to the concepts of Jewish mysticism, their religious and spiritual significance and how they relate to life today.
6 x 9, 224 pp, Quality PB, 978-1-58023-200-5 **$18.99**; HC, 978-1-58023-029-2 **$21.95**

The Way Into Jewish Prayer
By Lawrence A. Hoffman
Opens the door to 3,000 years of Jewish prayer, making available all anyone needs to feel at home in the Jewish way of communicating with God.
6 x 9, 208 pp, Quality PB, 978-1-58023-201-2 **$18.99**

Also Available: **The Way Into Jewish Prayer Teacher's Guide**
By Rabbi Jennifer Ossakow Goldsmith
8½ x 11, 42 pp, PB, 978-1-58023-345-3 **$8.99**
Visit our website to download a free copy.

The Way Into Judaism and the Environment
By Jeremy Benstein
Explores the ways in which Judaism contributes to contemporary social-environmental issues, the extent to which Judaism is part of the problem and how it can be part of the solution.
6 x 9, 288 pp, HC, 978-1-58023-268-5 **$24.99**

The Way Into *Tikkun Olam* (Repairing the World)
By Elliot N. Dorff
An accessible introduction to the Jewish concept of the individual's responsibility to care for others and repair the world.
6 x 9, 320 pp, HC, 978-1-58023-269-2 **$24.99**; 304 pp, Quality PB, 978-1-58023-328-6 **$18.99**

The Way Into Torah
By Norman J. Cohen
Helps guide in the exploration of the origins and development of Torah, explains why it should be studied and how to do it.
6 x 9, 176 pp, Quality PB, 978-1-58023-198-5 **$16.99**

The Way Into the Varieties of Jewishness
By Sylvia Barack Fishman, PhD
Explores the religious and historical understanding of what it has meant to be Jewish from ancient times to the present controversy over "Who is a Jew?"
6 x 9, 288 pp, HC, 978-1-58023-030-8 **$24.99**

Theology/Philosophy

A Touch of the Sacred: A Theologian's Informal Guide to Jewish Belief
By Dr. Eugene B. Borowitz and Frances W. Schwartz Explores the musings from the
leading theologian of liberal Judaism. 6 x 9, 256 pp, HC, 978-1-58023-337-8 **$21.99**

Talking about God: Exploring the Meaning of Religious Life with
Kierkegaard, Buber, Tillich and Heschel *By Daniel F. Polish, PhD*
Examines the meaning of the human religious experience with the greatest theolo-
gians of modern times. 6 x 9, 160 pp, HC, 978-1-59473-230-0 **$21.99** *(A SkyLight Paths book)*

Jews & Judaism in the 21st Century: Human Responsibility, the
Presence of God, and the Future of the Covenant
Edited by Rabbi Edward Feinstein; Foreword by Paula E. Hyman
Five celebrated leaders in Judaism examine contemporary Jewish life.
6 x 9, 192 pp, HC, 978-1-58023-315-6 **$24.99**

Christians and Jews in Dialogue: Learning in the Presence of the Other
By Mary C. Boys and Sara S. Lee; Foreword by Dr. Dorothy Bass
6 x 9, 240 pp, HC, 978-1-59473-144-0 **$21.99** *(A SkyLight Paths book)*

The Death of Death: Resurrection and Immortality in Jewish Thought
By Neil Gillman 6 x 9, 336 pp, Quality PB, 978-1-58023-081-0 **$18.95**

Ethics of the Sages: Pirke Avot—Annotated & Explained
Translation & Annotation by Rabbi Rami Shapiro
5½ x 8¼, 208 pp, Quality PB, 978-1-59473-207-2 **$16.99** *(A SkyLight Paths book)*

Hasidic Tales: Annotated & Explained
By Rabbi Rami Shapiro; Foreword by Andrew Harvey
5½ x 8¼, 240 pp, Quality PB, 978-1-893361-86-7 **$16.95** *(A SkyLight Paths Book)*

A Heart of Many Rooms: Celebrating the Many Voices within Judaism
By David Hartman 6 x 9, 352 pp, Quality PB, 978-1-58023-156-5 **$19.95**

The Hebrew Prophets: Selections Annotated & Explained
Translation & Annotation by Rabbi Rami Shapiro; Foreword by Zalman M. Schachter-Shalomi
5½ x 8¼, 224 pp, Quality PB, 978-1-59473-037-5 **$16.99** *(A SkyLight Paths book)*

A Jewish Understanding of the New Testament
By Rabbi Samuel Sandmel; Preface by Rabbi David Sandmel
5½ x 8¼, 368 pp, Quality PB, 978-1-59473-048-1 **$19.99** *(A SkyLight Paths book)*

Keeping Faith with the Psalms: Deepen Your Relationship with God Using the Book
of Psalms *By Daniel F. Polish* 6 x 9, 320 pp, Quality PB, 978-1-58023-300-2 **$18.99**

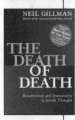

A Living Covenant: The Innovative Spirit in Traditional Judaism
By David Hartman 6 x 9, 368 pp, Quality PB, 978-1-58023-011-7 **$20.00**

Love and Terror in the God Encounter
The Theological Legacy of Rabbi Joseph B. Soloveitchik
By David Hartman 6 x 9, 240 pp, Quality PB, 978-1-58023-176-3 **$19.95**

The Personhood of God: Biblical Theology, Human Faith and the Divine Image
By Dr. Yochanan Muffs; Foreword by Dr. David Hartman 6 x 9, 240 pp, HC, 978-1-58023-265-4 **$24.99**

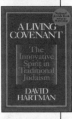

Traces of God: Seeing God in Torah, History and Everyday Life
By Neil Gillman 6 x 9, 240 pp, HC, 978-1-58023-249-4 **$21.99**

We Jews and Jesus: Exploring Theological Differences for Mutual Understanding
By Rabbi Samuel Sandmel; Preface by Rabbi David Sandmel
6 x 9, 176 pp, Quality PB, 978-1-59473-208-9 **$16.99** *(A SkyLight Paths book)*

Your Word Is Fire: The Hasidic Masters on Contemplative Prayer
Edited and translated by Arthur Green and Barry W. Holtz
6 x 9, 160 pp, Quality PB, 978-1-879045-25-5 **$15.95**

I Am Jewish
Personal Reflections Inspired by the Last Words of Daniel Pearl
Almost 150 Jews—both famous and not—from all walks of life, from all around
the world, write about many aspects of their Judaism.
Edited by Judea and Ruth Pearl
6 x 9, 304 pp, Deluxe PB w/flaps, 978-1-58023-259-3 **$18.99**
Download a free copy of the *I Am Jewish Teacher's Guide* at our website:
www.jewishlights.com

Congregation Resources

The Art of Public Prayer, 2nd Edition: Not for Clergy Only *By Lawrence A. Hoffman*
6 x 9, 272 pp, Quality PB, 978-1-893361-06-5 **$19.99** *(A SkyLight Paths book)*

Becoming a Congregation of Learners: Learning as a Key to Revitalizing
Congregational Life *By Isa Aron, PhD; Foreword by Rabbi Lawrence A. Hoffman*
6 x 9, 304 pp, Quality PB, 978-1-58023-089-6 **$19.95**

Finding a Spiritual Home: How a New Generation of Jews Can Transform the
American Synagogue *By Rabbi Sidney Schwarz*
6 x 9, 352 pp, Quality PB, 978-1-58023-185-5 **$19.95**

Jewish Pastoral Care, 2nd Edition: A Practical Handbook from Traditional &
Contemporary Sources *Edited by Rabbi Dayle A. Friedman*
6 x 9, 528 pp, HC, 978-1-58023-221-0 **$40.00**

Jewish Spiritual Direction: An Innovative Guide from Traditional and Contemporary
Sources *Edited by Rabbi Howard A. Addison and Barbara Eve Breitman*
6 x 9, 368 pp, HC, 978-1-58023-230-2 **$30.00**

The Self-Renewing Congregation: Organizational Strategies for Revitalizing
Congregational Life *By Isa Aron, PhD; Foreword by Dr. Ron Wolfson*
6 x 9, 304 pp, Quality PB, 978-1-58023-166-4 **$19.95**

Spiritual Community: The Power to Restore Hope, Commitment and Joy
By Rabbi David A. Teutsch, PhD 5½ x 8½, 144 pp, HC, 978-1-58023-270-8 **$19.99**

The Spirituality of Welcoming: How to Transform Your Congregation into a
Sacred Community *By Dr. Ron Wolfson* 6 x 9, 224 pp, Quality PB, 978-1-58023-244-9 **$19.99**

Rethinking Synagogues: A New Vocabulary for Congregational Life
By Rabbi Lawrence A. Hoffman 6 x 9, 240 pp, Quality PB, 978-1-58023-248-7 **$19.99**

Children's Books

What You Will See Inside a Synagogue
By Rabbi Lawrence A. Hoffman and Dr. Ron Wolfson; Full-color photos by Bill Aron
A colorful, fun-to-read introduction that explains the ways and whys of Jewish
worship and religious life. 8½ x 10½, 32 pp, Full-color photos, Quality PB, 978-1-59473-256-0 **$8.99**
For ages 6 & up (A SkyLight Paths book)

The Kids' Fun Book of Jewish Time
By Emily Sper 9 x 7½, 24 pp, Full-color illus., HC, 978-1-58023-311-8 **$16.99**

In God's Hands
By Lawrence Kushner and Gary Schmidt 9 x 12, 32 pp, HC, 978-1-58023-224-1 **$16.99**

Because Nothing Looks Like God
By Lawrence and Karen Kushner
Introduces children to the possibilities of spiritual life.
11 x 8½, 32 pp, Full-color illus., HC, 978-1-58023-092-6 **$17.99** *For ages 4 & up*

Also Available: **Because Nothing Looks Like God Teacher's Guide**
8½ x 11, 22 pp, PB, 978-1-58023-140-4 **$6.95** *For ages 5–8*

Board Book Companions to *Because Nothing Looks Like God*
5 x 5, 24 pp, Full-color illus., SkyLight Paths Board Books *For ages 0–4*

What Does God Look Like? 978-1-893361-23-2 **$7.99**

How Does God Make Things Happen? 978-1-893361-24-9 **$7.95**

Where Is God? 978-1-893361-17-1 **$7.99**

The Book of Miracles: A Young Person's Guide to Jewish Spiritual Awareness
By Lawrence Kushner. All-new illustrations by the author
6 x 9, 96 pp, 2-color illus., HC, 978-1-879045-78-1 **$16.95** *For ages 9 and up*

In Our Image: God's First Creatures
By Nancy Sohn Swartz 9 x 12, 32 pp, Full-color illus., HC, 978-1-879045-99-6 **$16.95** *For ages 4 & up*
Also Available as a Board Book: **How Did the Animals Help God?**
5 x 5, 24 pp, Board, Full-color illus., 978-1-59473-044-3 **$7.99** *For ages 0–4 (A SkyLight Paths book)*

What Makes Someone a Jew?
By Lauren Seidman
Reflects the changing face of American Judaism.
10 x 8½, 32 pp, Full-color photos, Quality PB Original, 978-1-58023-321-7 **$8.99** *For ages 3–6*

Meditation

The Handbook of Jewish Meditation Practices
A Guide for Enriching the Sabbath and Other Days of Your Life
By Rabbi David A. Cooper Easy-to-learn meditation techniques.
6 x 9, 208 pp, Quality PB, 978-1-58023-102-2 **$16.95**

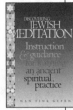

Discovering Jewish Meditation: Instruction & Guidance for Learning an Ancient
Spiritual Practice *By Nan Fink Gefen*
6 x 9, 208 pp, Quality PB, 978-1-58023-067-4 **$16.95**

A Heart of Stillness: A Complete Guide to Learning the Art of Meditation
By David A. Cooper 5½ x 8½, 272 pp, Quality PB, 978-1-893361-03-4 **$16.95** *(A SkyLight Paths book)*

Meditation from the Heart of Judaism: Today's Teachers Share Their Practices,
Techniques, and Faith *Edited by Avram Davis*
6 x 9, 256 pp, Quality PB, 978-1-58023-049-0 **$16.95**

Silence, Simplicity & Solitude: A Complete Guide to Spiritual Retreat at Home
By David A. Cooper 5½ x 8½, 336 pp, Quality PB, 978-1-893361-04-1 **$16.95**
(A SkyLight Paths book)

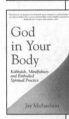

Ritual/Sacred Practice

The Jewish Dream Book: The Key to Opening the Inner Meaning of
Your Dreams *By Vanessa L. Ochs with Elizabeth Ochs; Full-color illus. by Kristina Swarner*
Instructions for how modern people can perform ancient Jewish dream practices
and dream interpretations drawn from the Jewish wisdom tradition.
8 x 8, 128 pp, Full-color illus., Deluxe PB w/flaps, 978-1-58023-132-9 **$16.95**

God in Your Body: Kabbalah, Mindfulness and Embodied Spiritual Practice
By Jay Michaelson
The first comprehensive treatment of the body in Jewish spiritual practice and an
essential guide to the sacred.
6 x 9, 288 pp, Quality PB, 978-1-58023-304-0 **$18.99**

The Book of Jewish Sacred Practices: CLAL's Guide to Everyday & Holiday
Rituals & Blessings *Edited by Rabbi Irwin Kula and Vanessa L. Ochs, PhD*
6 x 9, 368 pp, Quality PB, 978-1-58023-152-7 **$18.95**

Jewish Ritual: A Brief Introduction for Christians
By Rabbi Kerry M. Olitzky and Rabbi Daniel Judson
5½ x 8½, 144 pp, Quality PB, 978-1-58023-210-4 **$14.99**

The Rituals & Practices of a Jewish Life: A Handbook for Personal Spiritual
Renewal *Edited by Rabbi Kerry M. Olitzky and Rabbi Daniel Judson*
6 x 9, 272 pp, illus., Quality PB, 978-1-58023-169-5 **$18.95**

The Sacred Art of Lovingkindness: Preparing to Practice
By Rabbi Rami Shapiro 5½ x 8½, 176 pp, Quality PB, 978-1-59473-151-8 **$16.99**
(A SkyLight Paths book)

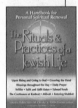

Science Fiction/Mystery & Detective Fiction

Mystery Midrash: An Anthology of Jewish Mystery & Detective Fiction
Edited by Lawrence W. Raphael; Preface by Joel Siegel
6 x 9, 304 pp, Quality PB, 978-1-58023-055-1 **$16.95**

Criminal Kabbalah: An Intriguing Anthology of Jewish Mystery & Detective Fiction
Edited by Lawrence W. Raphael; Foreword by Laurie R. King
6 x 9, 256 pp, Quality PB, 978-1-58023-109-1 **$16.95**

Wandering Stars: An Anthology of Jewish Fantasy & Science Fiction
Edited by Jack Dann; Introduction by Isaac Asimov
6 x 9, 272 pp, Quality PB, 978-1-58023-005-6 **$18.99**

More Wandering Stars: An Anthology of Outstanding Stories of Jewish Fantasy and
Science Fiction *Edited by Jack Dann; Introduction by Isaac Asimov*
6 x 9, 192 pp, Quality PB, 978-1-58023-063-6 **$16.95**

Holidays/Holy Days

Rosh Hashanah Readings: Inspiration, Information and Contemplation
Yom Kippur Readings: Inspiration, Information and Contemplation
Edited by Rabbi Dov Peretz Elkins with Section Introductions from Arthur Green's These Are the Words
An extraordinary collection of readings, prayers and insights that enable the modern worshiper to enter into the spirit of the High Holy Days in a personal and powerful way, permitting the meaning of the Jewish New Year to enter the heart.
RHR: 6 x 9, 400 pp, HC, 978-1-58023-239-5 **$24.99**
YKR: 6 x 9, 368 pp, HC, 978-1-58023-271-5 **$24.99**

Jewish Holidays: A Brief Introduction for Christians
By Rabbi Kerry M. Olitzky and Rabbi Daniel Judson
5½ x 8½, 144 pp, Quality PB, 978-1-58023-302-6 **$16.99**

Reclaiming Judaism as a Spiritual Practice: Holy Days and Shabbat
By Rabbi Goldie Milgram
7 x 9, 272 pp, Quality PB, 978-1-58023-205-0 **$19.99**

7th Heaven: Celebrating Shabbat with Rebbe Nachman of Breslov
By Moshe Mykoff with the Breslov Research Institute
5⅛ x 8¼, 224 pp, Deluxe PB w/flaps, 978-1-58023-175-6 **$18.95**

Shabbat, 2nd Edition: The Family Guide to Preparing for and Celebrating the Sabbath
By Dr. Ron Wolfson 7 x 9, 320 pp, illus., Quality PB, 978-1-58023-164-0 **$19.99**

Hanukkah, 2nd Edition: The Family Guide to Spiritual Celebration
By Dr. Ron Wolfson. Edited by Joel Lurie Grishaver.
7 x 9, 240 pp, illus., Quality PB, 978-1-58023-122-0 **$18.95**

The Jewish Family Fun Book, 2nd Edition: Holiday Projects, Everyday Activities, and Travel Ideas with Jewish Themes *By Danielle Dardashti and Roni Sarig. Illus. by Avi Katz.*
6 x 9, 304 pp, 70+ b/w illus. & diagrams, Quality PB, 978-1-58023-333-0 **$18.99**

The Jewish Lights Book of Fun Classroom Activities: Simple and Seasonal Projects for Teachers and Students *By Danielle Dardashti and Roni Sarig*
6 x 9, 240 pp, Quality PB, 978-1-58023-206-7 **$19.99**

Passover

My People's Passover Haggadah
Traditional Texts, Modern Commentaries
Edited by Rabbi Lawrence A. Hoffman, PhD, and David Arnow, PhD
A diverse and exciting collection of commentaries on the traditional Passover Haggadah—in two volumes!
Vol. 1: 7 x 10, 304 pp, HC, 978-1-58023-354-5 **$24.99**
Vol. 2: 7 x 10, 320 pp, HC, 978-1-58023-346-0 **$24.99**

Leading the Passover Journey
The Seder's Meaning Revealed, the Haggadah's Story Retold
By Rabbi Nathan Laufer
Uncovers the hidden meaning of the Seder's rituals and customs.
6 x 9, 224 pp, HC, 978-1-58023-211-1 **$24.99**

The Women's Passover Companion: Women's Reflections on the Festival of Freedom
Edited by Rabbi Sharon Cohen Anisfeld, Tara Mohr, and Catherine Spector
6 x 9, 352 pp, Quality PB, 978-1-58023-231-9 **$19.99**

The Women's Seder Sourcebook: Rituals & Readings for Use at the Passover Seder
Edited by Rabbi Sharon Cohen Anisfeld, Tara Mohr, and Catherine Spector
6 x 9, 384 pp, Quality PB, 978-1-58023-232-6 **$19.99**

Creating Lively Passover Seders: A Sourcebook of Engaging Tales, Texts & Activities
By David Arnow, PhD 7 x 9, 416 pp, Quality PB, 978-1-58023-184-8 **$24.99**

Passover, 2nd Edition: The Family Guide to Spiritual Celebration
By Dr. Ron Wolfson with Joel Lurie Grishaver 7 x 9, 352 pp, Quality PB, 978-1-58023-174-9 **$19.95**

Life Cycle
Marriage / Parenting / Family / Aging

The New Jewish Baby Album: Creating and Celebrating the Beginning of a Spiritual Life—A Jewish Lights Companion
By the Editors at Jewish Lights. Foreword by Anita Diamant. Preface by Rabbi Sandy Eisenberg Sasso.
A spiritual keepsake that will be treasured for generations. More than just a memory book, *shows you how—and why it's important*—to create a Jewish home and a Jewish life. 8 x 10, 64 pp, Deluxe Padded HC, Full-color illus., 978-1-58023-138-1 **$19.95**

The Jewish Pregnancy Book: A Resource for the Soul, Body & Mind during Pregnancy, Birth & the First Three Months
By Sandy Falk, MD, and Rabbi Daniel Judson, with Steven A. Rapp
Includes medical information, prayers and rituals for each stage of pregnancy, from a liberal Jewish perspective. 7 x 10, 208 pp, Quality PB, b/w photos, 978-1-58023-178-7 **$16.95**

Celebrating Your New Jewish Daughter: Creating Jewish Ways to Welcome Baby Girls into the Covenant—New and Traditional Ceremonies *By Debra Nussbaum Cohen; Foreword by Rabbi Sandy Eisenberg Sasso* 6 x 9, 272 pp, Quality PB, 978-1-58023-090-2 **$18.95**

The New Jewish Baby Book, 2nd Edition: Names, Ceremonies & Customs—A Guide for Today's Families *By Anita Diamant* 6 x 9, 336 pp, Quality PB, 978-1-58023-251-7 **$19.99**

Parenting as a Spiritual Journey: Deepening Ordinary and Extraordinary Events into Sacred Occasions *By Rabbi Nancy Fuchs-Kreimer*
6 x 9, 224 pp, Quality PB, 978-1-58023-016-2 **$16.95**

Parenting Jewish Teens: A Guide for the Perplexed
By Joanne Doades
Explores the questions and issues that shape the world in which today's Jewish teenagers live.
6 x 9, 200 pp, Quality PB, 978-1-58023-305-7 **$16.99**

Judaism for Two: A Spiritual Guide for Strengthening and Celebrating Your Loving Relationship *By Rabbi Nancy Fuchs-Kreimer and Rabbi Nancy H. Wiener; Foreword by Rabbi Elliot N. Dorff* Addresses the ways Jewish teachings can enhance and strengthen committed relationships. 6 x 9, 224 pp, Quality PB, 978-1-58023-254-8 **$16.99**

Embracing the Covenant: Converts to Judaism Talk About Why & How
By Rabbi Allan Berkowitz and Patti Moskovitz 6 x 9, 192 pp, Quality PB, 978-1-879045-50-7 **$16.95**

The Guide to Jewish Interfaith Family Life: An InterfaithFamily.com Handbook
Edited by Ronnie Friedland and Edmund Case 6 x 9, 384 pp, Quality PB, 978-1-58023-153-4 **$18.95**

Introducing My Faith and My Community
The Jewish Outreach Institute Guide for the Christian in a Jewish Interfaith Relationship
By Rabbi Kerry M. Olitzky 6 x 9, 176 pp, Quality PB, 978-1-58023-192-3 **$16.99**

Making a Successful Jewish Interfaith Marriage: The Jewish Outreach Institute Guide to Opportunities, Challenges and Resources *By Rabbi Kerry M. Olitzky with Joan Peterson Littman*
6 x 9, 176 pp, Quality PB, 978-1-58023-170-1 **$16.95**

The Creative Jewish Wedding Book: A Hands-On Guide to New & Old Traditions, Ceremonies & Celebrations *By Gabrielle Kaplan-Mayer*
9 x 9, 288 pp, b/w photos, Quality PB, 978-1-58023-194-7 **$19.99**

Divorce Is a Mitzvah: A Practical Guide to Finding Wholeness and Holiness When Your Marriage Dies *By Rabbi Perry Netter; Afterword by Rabbi Laura Geller.*
6 x 9, 224 pp, Quality PB, 978-1-58023-172-5 **$16.95**

A Heart of Wisdom: Making the Jewish Journey from Midlife through the Elder Years
Edited by Susan Berrin; Foreword by Harold Kushner
6 x 9, 384 pp, Quality PB, 978-1-58023-051-3 **$18.95**

So That Your Values Live On: Ethical Wills and How to Prepare Them
Edited by Jack Riemer and Nathaniel Stampfer
6 x 9, 272 pp, Quality PB, 978-1-879045-34-7 **$18.99**

Spirituality/Women's Interest

The Quotable Jewish Woman: Wisdom, Inspiration & Humor from the Mind & Heart
Edited and compiled by Elaine Bernstein Partnow
6 x 9, 496 pp, Quality PB, 978-1-58023-236-4 **$19.99**; HC, 978-1-58023-193-0 **$29.99**

The Divine Feminine in Biblical Wisdom Literature: Selections Annotated &
Explained *Translated and Annotated by Rabbi Rami Shapiro*
5½ x 8½, 240 pp, Quality PB, 978-1-59473-109-9 **$16.99** *(A SkyLight Paths book)*

The Women's Haftarah Commentary: New Insights from Women Rabbis on the
54 Weekly Haftarah Portions, the 5 Megillot & Special Shabbatot
Edited by Rabbi Elyse Goldstein 6 x 9, 560 pp, HC, 978-1-58023-133-6 **$39.99**

The Women's Torah Commentary: New Insights from Women Rabbis on the
54 Weekly Torah Portions *Edited by Rabbi Elyse Goldstein*
6 x 9, 496 pp, HC, 978-1-58023-076-6 **$34.95**

The Year Mom Got Religion: One Woman's Midlife Journey into Judaism
By Lee Meyerhoff Hendler 6 x 9, 208 pp, Quality PB, 978-1-58023-070-4 **$15.95**

See Holidays for *The Women's Passover Companion: Women's Reflections
on the Festival of Freedom* and *The Women's Seder Sourcebook: Rituals &
Readings for Use at the Passover Seder.* Also see Bar/Bat Mitzvah for *The
JGirl's Guide: The Young Jewish Woman's Handbook for Coming of Age.*

Spirituality / Crafts
(from SkyLight Paths, our sister imprint)

The Knitting Way: A Guide to Spiritual Self-Discovery
By Linda Skolnick and Janice MacDaniels
Shows how to use the practice of knitting to strengthen our spiritual selves.
7 x 9, 240 pp, Quality PB, 978-1-59473-079-5 **$16.99**

The Quilting Path: A Guide to Spiritual Self-Discovery through Fabric,
Thread and Kabbalah *By Louise Silk*
Explores how to cultivate personal growth through quilt making.
7 x 9, 192 pp, Quality PB, 978-1-59473-206-5 **$16.99**

The Painting Path: Embodying Spiritual Discovery through Yoga, Brush
and Color *By Linda Novick; Foreword by Richard Segalman*
Explores the divine connection you can experience through art.
7 x 9, 208 pp, 8-page full-color insert, Quality PB, 978-1-59473-226-3 **$18.99**

The Scrapbooking Journey: A Hands-On Guide to Spiritual Discovery
By Cory Richardson-Lauve; Foreword by Stacy Julian
Reveals how this craft can become a practice used to deepen and shape your life.
7 x 9, 176 pp, 8-page full-color insert, b/w photos, Quality PB, 978-1-59473-216-4 **$18.99**

Travel

Israel—A Spiritual Travel Guide, 2nd Edition
A Companion for the Modern Jewish Pilgrim
By Rabbi Lawrence A. Hoffman 4¾ x 10, 256 pp, Quality PB, illus., 978-1-58023-261-6 **$18.99**
Also Available: **The Israel Mission Leader's Guide** 978-1-58023-085-8 **$4.95**

12-Step

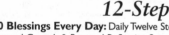

100 Blessings Every Day: Daily Twelve Step Recovery Affirmations, Exercises for
Personal Growth & Renewal Reflecting Seasons of the Jewish Year
By Rabbi Kerry M. Olitzky; Foreword by Rabbi Neil Gillman
4½ x 6½, 432 pp, Quality PB, 978-1-879045-30-9 **$16.99**

Recovery from Codependence: A Jewish Twelve Steps Guide to Healing Your Soul
By Rabbi Kerry M. Olitzky 6 x 9, 160 pp, Quality PB, 978-1-879045-32-3 **$13.95**

Twelve Jewish Steps to Recovery: A Personal Guide to Turning from Alcoholism &
Other Addictions—Drugs, Food, Gambling, Sex ...
By Rabbi Kerry M. Olitzky and Stuart A. Copans, MD; Preface by Abraham J. Twerski, MD
6 x 9, 144 pp, Quality PB, 978-1-879045-09-5 **$15.99**

Spirituality/Lawrence Kushner

Filling Words with Light: Hasidic and Mystical Reflections on Jewish Prayer
By Lawrence Kushner and Nehemia Polen
5½ x 8½, 176 pp, Quality PB, 978-1-58023-238-8 **$16.99**; HC, 978-1-58023-216-6 **$21.99**

The Book of Letters: A Mystical Hebrew Alphabet
Popular HC Edition, 6 x 9, 80 pp, 2-color text, 978-1-879045-00-2 **$24.95**
Collector's Limited Edition, 9 x 12, 80 pp, gold foil embossed pages, w/limited edition silkscreened
print, 978-1-879045-04-0 **$349.00**

The Book of Miracles: A Young Person's Guide to Jewish Spiritual Awareness
6 x 9, 96 pp, 2-color illus., HC, 978-1-879045-78-1 **$16.95** *For ages 9 and up*

The Book of Words: Talking Spiritual Life, Living Spiritual Talk
6 x 9, 160 pp, Quality PB, 978-1-58023-020-9 **$16.95**

Eyes Remade for Wonder: A Lawrence Kushner Reader *Introduction by Thomas Moore*
6 x 9, 240 pp, Quality PB, 978-1-58023-042-1 **$18.95**

God Was in This Place & I, i Did Not Know: Finding Self, Spirituality and
Ultimate Meaning 6 x 9, 192 pp, Quality PB, 978-1-879045-33-0 **$16.95**

Honey from the Rock: An Introduction to Jewish Mysticism
6 x 9, 176 pp, Quality PB, 978-1-58023-073-5 **$16.95**

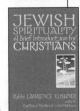

Invisible Lines of Connection: Sacred Stories of the Ordinary
5½ x 8½, 160 pp, Quality PB, 978-1-879045-98-9 **$15.95**

Jewish Spirituality—A Brief Introduction for Christians
5½ x 8½, 112 pp, Quality PB, 978-1-58023-150-3 **$12.95**

The River of Light: Jewish Mystical Awareness
6 x 9, 192 pp, Quality PB, 978-1-58023-096-4 **$16.95**

The Way Into Jewish Mystical Tradition
6 x 9, 224 pp, Quality PB, 978-1-58023-200-5 **$18.99**; HC, 978-1-58023-029-2 **$21.95**

Spirituality/Prayer

My People's Passover Haggadah: Traditional Texts, Modern Commentaries
Edited by Rabbi Lawrence A. Hoffman, PhD, and David Arnow, PhD Diverse commentaries
on the traditional Passover Haggadah—in two volumes! Vol. 1: 7 x 10, 304 pp, HC
978-1-58023-354-5 **$24.99** Vol. 2: 7 x 10, 320 pp, HC, 978-1-58023-346-0 **$24.99**

Witnesses to the One: The Spiritual History of the *Sh'ma* By Rabbi Joseph B. Meszler;
Foreword by Rabbi Elyse Goldstein 6 x 9, 176 pp, HC, 978-1-58023-309-5 **$19.99**

My People's Prayer Book Series

Traditional Prayers, Modern Commentaries *Edited by Rabbi Lawrence A. Hoffman*
Provides diverse and exciting commentary to the traditional liturgy, helping modern
men and women find new wisdom in Jewish prayer, and bring liturgy into their lives.
Each book includes Hebrew text, modern translation, and commentaries from all
perspectives of the Jewish world.

Vol. 1—The Sh'ma and Its Blessings
 7 x 10, 168 pp, HC, 978-1-879045-79-8 **$24.99**

Vol. 2—The Amidah
 7 x 10, 240 pp, HC, 978-1-879045-80-4 **$24.95**

Vol. 3—P'sukei D'zimrah (Morning Psalms)
 7 x 10, 240 pp, HC, 978-1-879045-81-1 **$24.95**

Vol. 4—Seder K'riat Hatorah (The Torah Service)
 7 x 10, 264 pp, HC, 978-1-879045-82-8 **$23.95**

Vol. 5—Birkhot Hashachar (Morning Blessings)
 7 x 10, 240 pp, HC, 978-1-879045-83-5 **$24.95**

Vol. 6—Tachanun and Concluding Prayers
 7 x 10, 240 pp, HC, 978-1-879045-84-2 **$24.95**

Vol. 7—Shabbat at Home
 7 x 10, 240 pp, HC, 978-1-879045-85-9 **$24.95**

Vol. 8—Kabbalat Shabbat (Welcoming Shabbat in the Synagogue)
 7 x 10, 240 pp, HC, 978-1-58023-121-3 **$24.99**

Vol. 9—Welcoming the Night: Minchah and Ma'ariv (Afternoon and
 Evening Prayer) 7 x 10, 272 pp, HC, 978-1-58023-262-3 **$24.99**

Vol. 10—Shabbat Morning: Shacharit and Musaf (Morning and
 Additional Services) 7 x 10, 240 pp, HC, 978-1-58023-240-1 **$24.99**

Spirituality

Journeys to a Jewish Life: Inspiring Stories from the Spiritual Journeys of American Jews *By Paula Amann*
Examines the soul treks of Jews lost and found. 6 x 9, 208 pp, HC, 978-1-58023-317-0 **$19.99**

The Adventures of Rabbi Harvey: A Graphic Novel of Jewish Wisdom and Wit in the Wild West *By Steve Sheinkin*
Jewish and American folktales combine in this witty and original graphic novel collection. Creatively retold and set on the western frontier of the 1870s.
6 x 9, 144 pp, Full-color illus., Quality PB, 978-1-58023-310-1 **$16.99**
Also Available: **The Adventures of Rabbi Harvey Teacher's Guide**
8½ x 11, 32 pp, PB, 978-1-58023-326-2 **$8.99**

Ethics of the Sages: *Pirke Avot*—Annotated & Explained
Translation and Annotation by Rabbi Rami Shapiro
5½ x 8½, 192 pp, Quality PB, 978-1-59473-207-2 **$16.99** *(A SkyLight Paths book)*

A Book of Life: Embracing Judaism as a Spiritual Practice
By Michael Strassfeld 6 x 9, 528 pp, Quality PB, 978-1-58023-247-0 **$19.99**

Meaning and Mitzvah: Daily Practices for Reclaiming Judaism through Prayer, God, Torah, Hebrew, Mitzvot and Peoplehood *By Rabbi Goldie Milgram*
7 x 9, 336 pp, Quality PB, 978-1-58023-256-2 **$19.99**

The Soul of the Story: Meetings with Remarkable People
By Rabbi David Zeller 6 x 9, 288 pp, HC, 978-1-58023-272-2 **$21.99**

Aleph-Bet Yoga: Embodying the Hebrew Letters for Physical and Spiritual Well-Being
By Steven A. Rapp. Foreword by Tamar Frankiel, PhD and Judy Greenfeld. Preface by Hart Lazer.
7 x 10, 128 pp, b/w photos, Quality PB, Layflat binding, 978-1-58023-162-6 **$16.95**

Does the Soul Survive? A Jewish Journey to Belief in Afterlife, Past Lives & Living with Purpose *By Rabbi Elie Kaplan Spitz; Foreword by Brian L Weiss, MD*
6 x 9, 288 pp, Quality PB, 978-1-58023-165-7 **$16.99**

First Steps to a New Jewish Spirit: Reb Zalman's Guide to Recapturing the Intimacy & Ecstasy in Your Relationship with God *By Rabbi Zalman M. Schachter-Shalomi with Donald Gropman* 6 x 9, 144 pp, Quality PB, 978-1-58023-182-4 **$16.95**

God in Our Relationships: Spirituality between People from the Teachings of Martin Buber *By Rabbi Dennis S. Ross* 5½ x 8½, 160 pp, Quality PB, 978-1-58023-147-3 **$16.95**

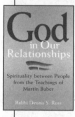

Judaism, Physics and God: Searching for Sacred Metaphors in a Post-Einstein World
By Rabbi David W. Nelson 6 x 9, 368 pp, Quality PB, inc. reader's discussion guide, 978-1-58023-306-4 **$18.99**;
HC, 352 pp, 978-1-58023-252-4 **$24.99**

The Jewish Lights Spirituality Handbook: A Guide to Understanding, Exploring & Living a Spiritual Life *Edited by Stuart M. Matlins*
What exactly is "Jewish" about spirituality? How do I make it a part of my life? Fifty of today's foremost spiritual leaders share their ideas and experience with us.
6 x 9, 456 pp, Quality PB, 978-1-58023-093-3 **$19.99**

Bringing the Psalms to Life: How to Understand and Use the Book of Psalms
By Daniel F. Polish 6 x 9, 208 pp, Quality PB, 978-1-58023-157-2 **$16.95**;
HC, 978-1-58023-077-3 **$21.95**

God & the Big Bang: Discovering Harmony between Science & Spirituality
By Daniel C. Matt 6 x 9, 216 pp, Quality PB, 978-1-879045-89-7 **$16.99**

Minding the Temple of the Soul: Balancing Body, Mind, and Spirit through Traditional Jewish Prayer, Movement, and Meditation *By Tamar Frankiel, PhD, and Judy Greenfeld*
7 x 10, 184 pp, illus., Quality PB, 978-1-879045-64-4 **$16.95**
Audiotape of the Blessings and Meditations: 60 min. **$9.95**
Videotape of the Movements and Meditations: 46 min. **$20.00**

One God Clapping: The Spiritual Path of a Zen Rabbi *By Alan Lew with Sherril Jaffe*
5½ x 8½, 336 pp, Quality PB, 978-1-58023-115-2 **$16.95**

There Is No Messiah ... and You're It: The Stunning Transformation of Judaism's Most Provocative Idea *By Rabbi Robert N. Levine, DD*
6 x 9, 192 pp, Quality PB, 978-1-58023-255-5 **$16.99**

These Are the Words: A Vocabulary of Jewish Spiritual Life
By Arthur Green 6 x 9, 304 pp, Quality PB, 978-1-58023-107-7 **$18.95**